A BATTLE SCENE AT POINT PLEASANT OCTOBER 10, 1774.

A facsimile of the bas-relief on the western side of the Battle Monument, at Point Pleasant, West Virginia.

HISTORY

OF THE

BATTLE OF POINT PLEASANT

FOUGHT BETWEEN WHITE MEN AND INDIANS

AT THE

MOUTH OF THE GREAT KANAWHA RIVER,

(Now Point Pleasant, West Virginia.)

MONDAY, OCTOBER 10th, 1774.

THE CHIEF EVENT OF LORD DUNMORE'S WAR.

BY

VIRGIL A. LEWIS, A. M.

(STATE HISTORIAN AND ARCHIVIST.)

Member of the American Historical Association—Member of the American Political Science
Association—Member of the National Geographic Society—Member Mississippi
Valley Historical Association—Member of the Ohio Valley Historical
Association—Author of "History of West Virginia," etc.

(Abridged from the Author's Manuscript "History of Lord Dunmore's War.")

"Roll back—my soul—to the times of my Fathers. * * * There comes a voice that
awakes my soul—It is the voice of days that are gone—They roll before me with all their
deeds."—OSSIAN.

CHARLESTON,
THE TRIBUNE PRINTING COMPANY,
WEST VIRGINIA,
1909.

Notice

In many older books, foxing (or discoloration) occurs and, in some instances, print lightens with wear and age. Reprinted books, such as this, often duplicate these flaws, notwithstanding efforts to reduce or eliminate them. The pages of this reprint have been digitally enhanced and, where possible, the flaws eliminated in order to provide clarity of content and a pleasant reading experience.

History of the Battle of Point Pleasant;
Fought Between White Men and Indians at the Mouth of the
Great Kanawha River, (Now Point Pleasant, West Virginia.)
Monday, October 10th, 1774.
The Chief Event of Lord Dunmore's War.

Copyright © 1909 Virgil A. Lewis

Originally published
Charleston, West Virginia
1909

Reprinted by:

Janaway Publishing, Inc.
732 Kelsey Ct.
Santa Maria, California 93454
(805) 925-1038
www.janawaygenealogy.com

2010

ISBN 10: 1-59641-203-8
ISBN 13: 978-1-59641-203-3

Made in the United States of America

A PREFATORY NOTE.

I was born within a few miles of the battle-field of Point Pleasant, the chief event of Lord Dunmore's War, and reared largely among the descendants of the men who participated in that struggle. It was therefore but natural that even in my early years there was awakened an interest in the history not only of the battle itself, but of all that related to the participants therein—to all that concerned the gallantry and achievements of the men of 1774. In my research I have sought to collect material from trust-worthy sources, because I have desired to give to this work the interest which every reader must have in a work treating of history. For this reason the only material used has been drawn from original sources, documents, and writings which were contemporaneous with the occurrence of the events described. Much error has been incorporated into the later writings regarding Dunmore's War. This is the result of a carelessness on the part of those, who without making research and investigation necessary to arrive at truth, seized rumors, traditions, and vague recollections, as sufficient authority upon which to base an assertion, and who substituted their own inferences for authenticated facts. These errors of statement have sometimes been repeated by considerate writers whose distrust was not excited; and this has increased the difficulties of pains-taking historians. But now, the publication of Thwaites and Kellogg's "Documentary History of Dunmore's War;" the "Revolution on the Upper Ohio," by the same authors; the printing by Virginia of the Journals of the House of Burgesses; Ford's reprint of the Journals of the Continental Congress and other sources of recent appearance, added to that which was previously available, has almost given to Dunmore's War a literature of its own. It is therefore, to be hoped that, henceforth, writers who heretofore, indulged in what may be termed the gossip of history, may no longer accept myths, legends and traditions as authority, and that they will thus cease to perpetuate the errors of statements long current, regarding Lord Dunmore's War and its chief event—the battle of Point Pleasant.

V. A. L.

Charleston, West Virginia,
    September 1, 1909.

TABLE OF CONTENTS.

CHAPTER I.

THE VIRGINIA FRONTIER IN 1774—THE INDIAN NATIONS OF THE OHIO WILDER-
NESS.

First White Settlements west of the Blue Ridge—County Organization west
of that Mountain Barrier—A Savage Empire—The Confederated Indian Nations Northwest of the Ohio—The Shawnees, Miamis, Ottowas,
Delawares, Wyandots, and Mingoes ....Pages 5—13

CHAPTER II.

LORD DUNMORE'S WAR—ITS CAUSES.

The War on the Frontier—First Plan of Campaign—The Ohio River to be
the Line of Defensive Operations—Second Plan for Prosecution of the
War—A Preliminary Movement—Erection of Fort Fincastle at Wheel-
ing—Expedition of Major Angus McDonald into the Ohio Wilderness—
Instructions to General Andrew Lewis to erect a Fort at the Mouth
of the Great Kanawha River—Lord Dunmore Leaves Williamsburg—
Crosses the Blue Ridge—Organizes the Northern Division of an Army
—Commands it in Person—Its Westward March to the Ohio River....
Pages 14—23

CHAPTER III.

THE SOUTHERN DIVISION OR LEFT WING OF THE ARMY.

General Andrew Lewis ordered by Lord Dunmore to collect the Southern
Wing of the Army—Recruiting Stations in the Counties of Augusta,
Botetourt and Fincastle—Gathering of the Army at "Camp Union" on
the Big Levels of Greenbrier—Official Organization of the Augusta
County Regiment; of the Botetourt County Regiment, and of the Fincastle County Battalion—Independent Companies—The Minute Men
from Culpeper County—The Dunmore County Volunteers—The Bedford County Riflemen—The Kentucky Pioneers.........Pages 24—29

CHAPTER IV.

THE WESTWARD MARCH OF THE SOUTHERN DIVISION FROM CAMP UNION TO THE
OHIO RIVER.

Westward March of the Augusta County Regiment—The Botetourt County
Regiment leaves Camp Union—Colonel Christian with the Fincastle
County Battalion brings up the Rear—Captain Anthony Bledsoe with
his Company, and the Sick of the Army, left at Camp Union—Location
of Encampments, all the way from Camp Union to Camp Point Pleasant at the Mouth of the Great Kanawha River.........Pages 30—39

CHAPTER V.

THE BATTLE OF POINT PLEASANT.

Disposition of the Virginian Army in the Ohio Valley on the Battle Eve—
The Early Morning Attack—Account of the Battle, written on the
Field by Lieutenant Isaac Shelby—Account written by Colonel William Fleming commanding the Botetourt County Regiment—Account
written by Captain John Stuart, a Participant in the Battle—The
Killed and Wounded—Accounts of the Battle published in the Colonies
and throughout Europe ....Pages 40—53

CHAPTER VI.

THE VIRGINIAN ARMY IN THE OHIO WILDERNESS.

March of the Northern Division-of the Army under Dunmore from Fort
Gower to the Pickaway Plains—Advance of the Southern Division
under General Lewis from Point Pleasant into the Scioto Valley—Pre-
liminary Treaty of "Camp Charlotte"—The Terms agreed upon—Re-
turn of the Army—Garrisons left at Point Pleasant, Wheeling and
Pittsburg—The Supplemental Treaty at Pittsburg in 1775—Complete
Confirmation and Ratification of the Terms of the Treaty of "Camp
Charlotte"—Indian Nations in amity with Virginia and the New
American Nation as well ....Pages 54—66

CHAPTER VII.

THE INFLUENCE OF THE BATTLE OF POINT PLEASANT UPON THE SUBSEQUENT HISTORY OF THE UNITED STATES.

Treaties of Camp Charlotte and Pittsburg kept Indians quiet for four
years—General Gates thereby enabled to collect American soldiery
and overthrow Burgoyne at Saratoga—This meant France to the
Rescue—Enabled Frontiersmen to Settle Kentucky in 1775—A base of
operations for General George Rogers Clark in his Illinois Campaign—Illinois County created by the General Assembly of Virginia—
The Mississippi River, and not the Alleghenies, made the western
Boundary of the United States in 1783 ....Pages 67—69

CHAPTER VIII.

PAY OF THE SOLDIERS IN DUNMORE'S WAR—TOTAL EXPENSES OF THAT WAR— HOW THEY WERE PAID.

Lord Dunmore recommends Payment of Troops—Action of the Virginia
Assembly in the Matter—Ordinance of the Convention in July 1775—
Commissioners appointed to adjust all Claims of the War—Full pay-
ment made—Total cost of the War ....Pages 70—74

CHAPTER IX.

HISTORY AND DESCRIPTION OF THE POINT PLEASANT BATTLE MONUMENT.

The Historic Field long Unmarked—Description of the Battlefield in 1827 —Resolutions of Hon. James M. Laidley in the Virginia Assembly in 1849—The Point Pleasant Monument Association Incorporated in 1860—The Centennial Celebration in 1874—First State Appropriation for a Monument—The Fund Loaned at Interest while the years passed away—Trustees appointed—The Work Begun—Further State Appropriations—Aid from the National Government—The Monument Completed—Its Dimensions ....Pages 75—82

CHAPTER X.

HISTORY VERSUS TRADITION—TRUTH VERSUS ERROR.

Error of Statement—Innocence of Captain Michael Cresap—Integrity and honesty of purpose of Lord Dunmore—Contemporary Documents showing the estimation in which he was held by the Virginians—The Soldierly Character of General Andrew Lewis ....Pages 83—95

CHAPTER XI.

POETRY OF THE BATTLE OF POINT PLEASANT.

The Camp Song at Point Pleasant—The Shawnee Battle on the Banks of the Ohio—The Battle Song of the Great Kanawha—Battle of Point Pleasant: A Centennial Ode ....Pages 96—102

CHAPTER XII.

THE MURDER OF CORNSTALK AT POINT PLEASANT, NOVEMBER 10, 1777.

Cornstalk, the Shawnee Chieftain, with Red-Hawk a Delaware Chief, visits Point Pleasant in the Autumn of 1777—Brings intelligence that his People will violate terms of the Treaties of Camp Charlotte and Pittsburg, and join the British—Is detained by Captain Arbuckle, commandant at Fort Randolph—Is joined by his son Ellinipsico—All are killed by enraged Virginians—The Account written by Captain John Stuart, who was an eye-witness of the Tragedy—Addenda.......
Pages 103—109

APPENDIX A.

THE ONLY ROSTERS PRESERVED OF THE COMPANIES WHICH WERE IN THE BATTLE
OF POINT PLEASANT, OR ARRIVED WITH COLONEL CHRISTIAN AFTER
IT HAD BEEN FOUGHT AND WON.

Captain William Nalle's Company of the Augusta Regiment—The Companies of Captains John Murray, Philip Love, John Lewis, John Stuart, Robert McClennahan, and Henry Pauling, of the Botetourt Regiment —The Companies of Captains Evan Shelby, William Campbell and James Harrod of the Fincastle County Battalion—Captain Thomas Buford's Bedford County Riflemen ....Pages 110-120

APPENDIX B.

THE AFTER-LIFE OF THE MEN WHO FOUGHT THE BATTLE OF POINT PLEASANT.

Their Services in the War for Independence—Their Services in the Civil Life of our Country—Their names preserved in those of Counties and Towns—A Monument to their Memory ....Pages 121—122

APPENDIX C.

EXTRACTS FROM THE VIRGINIA GAZETTE RELATING TO LORD DUNMORE'S WAR.

Indian atrocities on the Frontier—Governor Dunmore leaves Williamsburg for the Western Border—Mustering of the Two Divisions of the Army—The first Printed Account of the Battle of Point Pleasant—Results of the War ....Pages 123—127

APPENDIX D.

A PARTIAL LIST OF THE MEN WOUNDED IN THE BATTLE OF POINT PLEASANT, WHO WERE AFTERWARD GRANTED PENSIONS BY THE COMMONWEALTH OF VIRGINIA.

Names of wounded Men—How wounded—Organization to which each belonged—Amount of Pension granted each—For what time to continue
Pages 128—129

APPENDIX E.

KINSHIP OF THE MEN WHO FOUGHT THE BATTLE OF POINT PLEASANT.

Men who were of Blood-Kin—Those connected by Marriage—A Remarkable Record ....Pages 130—131

LIST OF ILLUSTRATIONS.

I. FRONTISPIECE, A Battle Scene at Point Pleasant, October 10, 1774 —Facsimile of the Bas-Relief on the lower Plinth on the western side of the Battle Monument.

II. Portrait of Lord Dunmore. Opposite page 14.

III. Portrait of Major Angus McDonald. Opposite page 20.

IV. The Point Pleasant Battle Monument. Opposite page 75.

V. The Cornstalk Monument at Point Pleasant. Opposite page 103.

HISTORY OF THE BATTLE OF POINT PLEASANT.

CHAPTER I.

THE VIRGINIA FRONTIER IN 1774—THE INDIAN NATIONS OF THE OHIO WILDERNESS.

"An opinion had long prevailed that these mountains presented an everlasting barrier to the ambition of the Whites. Their great height, their prodigious extent, their rugged and horrid appearance suggested to the imagination unfeigned images of terror. The wolf, the bear, the panther, and the Indian, were the tenants of these forlorn and inaccessible precipices."—Burk's *"History of Virginia,"* Vol. II, p. 331.

"Our immediate predecessors in the occupancy of Ohio where the Shawnees, Miamis, Delawares and Ottawas of the Algonquin linguistic stock and the Wyandots and Mingoes of the Iroquois linguistic family."—*"Ohio Archæological and Historical Society Publications."*—Vol. VI., p. 75.

WHITE SETTLERS WEST OF THE BLUE RIDGE:—For a number of years after the founding of Jamestown the white settlements were confined to the banks of the James River. In time they extended over the Tide-Water Region; and thence into the Piedmont Region even to the base of the Blue Ridge. Explorers made known the region beyond and civilized men crossed this great mountain barrier, and found homes in the beautiful Shenandoah Valley. The first to do this were Adam Miller and Morgan Morgan who came in 1726. The next year a number of Germans from Pennsylvania, in quest of fertile lands, crossed the Potomac at what is now known as the "Old Pack-Horse Ford," and a mile above it on its southern bank, founded a little village which they called New Mecklenberg—now Shepherdstown. In 1732, Joist Hite brought sixteen families from York, Pennsylvania, all of whom settled in the Shenandoah Valley. Speedily other white men found homes along the Upper Potomac, and in the South Branch Valley. In 1731, John Lewis, John Mackey, and others came to the Upper Shenandoah Valley. In 1736 Governor Gooch issued a patent for 118,000 acres of land including the settlement of John Lewis, to William Beverley, John Robinson and others. All surrendered their interests to Beverley, and the survey came to be known as "Beverly Manor."[1] Within it, in 1748, the town of Staunton was established by law, and received its name in honor of Lady Gooch, wife of the Governor, whose maiden name was Staunton. This was the first home of Cavalier civilization west of the Blue Ridge. In 1736, Benjamin Borden, of New Jersey, visited the Upper Shenandoah Valley; and so pleased with the region was he, that he applied to and received from Governor Gooch a grant for 500,000 acres, chiefly in what is now Rockbridge county, Virginia. Borden went to Europe the next year, and returned with a hundred families— Irish, Scotch-Irish—from the north of Ireland all of whom settled on his lands. As early as 1732 two cabins were standing at the "Old Shawnee Springs" in the Lower Shenandoah Valley. In 1743 James Wood had laid out twenty-six lots, and the House of Burgesses that year established the town of Winchester—another center of Cavalier civilization. In 1745 Thomas, Sixth Lord Fairfax, whose Land Patent embraced the whole of the Lower Shenandoah Valley and extended westward to the South Branch of the Potomac, came to Virginia and having employed young George Washington to survey these lands, in quantities to suit purchasers, established his home at "Greenway Court" thirteen miles southeast of Winchester, and did all he could to induce immigration to his lands. Thus did civilized men find homes west of the Blue Ridge. Hither came and here met the devoted Hugenot, the pious Cavalier of Virginia, the strict Catholic of Maryland, the steady Quaker of Pennsylvania, the Baptists and Presbyterians from New Jersey, the sternly religious Puritans from New England and the Lutherans and Moravians from the banks of the Rhine. For awhile these distinct elements maintained their individuality, but a long series of Indian wars, forced them into a united whole. From these settlements in the valleys of the Shenandoah, others rapidly extended westward to the valleys and highlands of the Allegheny mountains; thence westward they advanced along the trans-Allegheny rivers, to the Tygart's Valley river, to the West Fork river and its tributaries; thence down the Monongahela to Fort Pitt, and to the Ohio at Wheeling, Moundsville, mouth of Fishing creek, and Letart Falls; around the upper waters of the

---

1. See Waddell's "Annals of Augusta County," p. 14-38.

Little Kanawha, and to the Valley of the Greenbrier river; the upper waters of New river; and thence to and down the valleys of the Clinch and Holston rivers. Such was the Virginia Frontier west of the Blue Ridge in 1774, where, as is believed, forty thousand white people—men, women and children—were residing in cabin homes between Fort Pitt and the source of the Tennessee river.

COUNTY ORGANIZATION WEST OF THE BLUE RIDGE:—In 1634 the Colony of Virginia was divided in eight counties or shires similar to those of England. Henceforth Virginia ever tried to keep civil government abreast of her most adventurous pioneers, and her House of Burgesses—the legislative body of the Colony—continued to pass acts creating new counties, until in 1734, thirty-three of these were checkered on her map, all east of the Blue Ridge.

From 1734 to 1738, all the territory of Virginia west of that mountain barrier was deemed to be in Orange county created in the former year. In the latter, an Act was passed creating the counties of Augusta and Frederick—both west of the Blue Ridge—to include all "the uttermost parts of Virginia," even to the Mississippi. It was stated in this Act that "great numbers of people had settled themselves of late upon the waters of the Shenandoah, Opequon, and South Branch of the Potomac, and the branches thereof, on the northwest side of the Blue Ridge." These two counties were divided by a line drawn from the head spring of Hedgman's River at the Blue Ridge to the source of the North Branch of the Potomac, Frederick county being to northward and Augusta to the southward thereof.[2]

In 1753 it was shown to the House of Burgesses that Frederick county was "a very long and large extent, and therefore inconvenient to the inhabitants thereof," and it was enacted that all that part of said county, westward of the Great North Mountain and Warm Spring Mountain should henceforth be a distinct county to be called and known by the name of Hampshire county.[3]

In 1769, a petition numerously signed by the inhabitants of the southern part of Augusta county, set forth to the Burgesses "that many inconveniences attended the inhabitants of the county of

2. Hening's "Statutes at Large," Vol. V., pp. 78-80.
3. Hening's "Statutes at Large," Vol. VI., p. 376.

Augusta, by reason of the great extent thereof;" and an Act was passed that year dividing Augusta by a line beginning at the Blue Ridge and running thence north fifty-five degrees west as far as the Courts of the two counties should extend it. If extended to the confines of Virginia, it would have crossed Greenbrier river about five miles below the present town of Marlinton in Pocahontas county, and would have reached the Ohio river at or near where Bellville in the present county of Wood, in West Virginia, now stands. All that portion of Augusta north of this line retained the name of Augusta; and all that part south thereof, received the name of Botetourt county. A section of the Act creating this county provided that "because the people situated on the waters of the Mississippi, in the said county of Botetourt, will be very remote from the county-seat, they shall be exempt from the payment of taxes for the purpose of building a court-house and prison for the county."[4]

In a preamble to an Act of the Burgesses passed in 1772, it was explained that the settlers on the waters of the Holston and New rivers in the county of Botetourt "labor under great inconveniencies by reason of the extent of the said county." It was therefore enacted that Botetourt be divided by the Great Kanawha and New rivers, and that all that part southwest of said streams should be called and known as Fincastle county.[5]

The same year it was made to appear to the Burgesses that many of the inhabitants of Frederick county suffered great inconvenience because of the extent of this county, and by an Act passed—1772—it was divided into three parts, the central portion retaining the name of Frederick; the southern part receiving the name of Dunmore county; and the northern part, that of Berkeley county.[6]

About this time all the northern part of Augusta county west of Hampshire to the Monongahela and Upper Ohio Valleys, even beyond Fort Pitt—a region having at that time an undefined boundary—came to be known as the "District of West Augusta." It was the home of many as brave men as ever dared the perils of a wilderness.

Such was the county organization of Virginia west of the Blue

4.   Hening's "Statutes at Large," Vol. VIII., pp. 394-398.
5.   Hening's "Statutes at Large," Vol. VIII., pp. 600, 601.
6.   Hening's "Statutes at Large," Vol. VIII., p. 597.

Ridge in 1774—Augusta, Botetourt and Fincastle to the west and southwest—and Frederick, Dunmore, Berkeley and Hampshire to the northeast, all together with the "District of West Augusta," embracing the present states of West Virginia, and Kentucky, and all with undefined boundaries, Virginia's portion of the old Northwest Territory beyond the Ohio. At this time the fertile Shenandoah Valley had been largely brought under cultivation and thousands of domestic cattle ranged the forest lands adjoining the plantations. A like condition existed in the adjacent river valleys to the westward.

A SAVAGE EMPIRE.

The Virginia Frontiersmen in 1774 were dwelling upon the borderland of a savage empire, the boundary of which they had been forcing back for many years. By the treaty of Albany in 1720 the Blue Ridge was agreed upon as the boundary line between the possessions of white and red men. In 1744, by that of Lancaster, this was made an imaginary line extending from the Potomac through the sites of the present cities of Martinsburg, Winchester and Staunton, in the Shenandoah Valley. At the treaty of Fort Stanwix— now Rome, New York,—between the English representative, Sir William Johnson and the Six Nations—Cayugas, Onondagas, Onedias, Senecas, Mohawks, and Tuscaroras—the Ohio was made the boundary, the title to all the region east of that river being transferred to the King of England. From it the tribes that once dwelt therein had previously removed. The Kanawhas had gone from the upper tributaries of the river which bears their name, to join their kinsmen, the Iroquois in New York; the Shawnees had abandoned the Indian Old Fields of the valley of the South Branch of the Potomac; the Delawares were gone from the valley of the Monongahela; the Cherokees who claimed all the region between the Great Kanawha and Big Sandy rivers, had never occupied it. The Indian Nations who were to be history makers in their wars with the Virginians, were dwellers in the Ohio Wilderness. These were as follows:— Miamis, Ottawas, Shawnees, Delawares, Wyandots and Mingoes.

The Miamis were a powerful nation whose habitat was in the

region drained by the great Miami and Maumee rivers. Their ancient name was "Twightwee," and they claimed to be the original proprietors of the lands they occupied—that they had always had them. They were the only Indians that ever waged successful war with the Six Nations. This ended in 1702 by a council between the two belligerant powers.[7]

They were a warlike people, and were much of the time in broils with their neighbors. In 1763, they removed from Piqua, their chief town, the site of which is now in Miami county, Ohio, to the Miami of the Lakes.

The Shawnees were the most remarkable of all the people inhabiting the region east of the Mississippi. Thirty-one of them were present at the treaty with William Penn, at Shackamaxon in 1682. Soon thereafter, they fell under the rule of the Six Nations, and, henceforth, for more than half a century they existed in branches in various regions. Some of them occupied the Lower Shenandoah Valley, where they had a town at "Shawnee Springs" now Winchester, Virginia; at one time the hunting grounds of the principal part of them were in Kentucky; thence they removed to the valleys of the Cumberland and Tennessee rivers, but were forced by the Cherokees to abandon this region; and four hundred of them, in 1678, found a home on the Mobile river, in New Spain; where, in 1745 they had four hundred and fifty warriors. Four hundred more leaving the Mississippi Valley, settled on the Congaree river in South Carolina. Seventy families later, removed from here to the valley of the Susquehanna in Pennsylvania; others followed, and in 1732 there were seven hundred and fifty Shawnee warriors on that river. But now there was to be a gathering of all the Shawnee people. Their future home was to be on the Scioto, where, on the Pickaway Plains, the "Wilderness Garden" of the valley of that river, their principal towns were located. Here, prior to 1760, the nation was completely reunited. It was composed of four tribes or branches—the *Piqua,* men born in ashes; the *Kiskapoke,* men of war; the *Mequacheke,* the fat men; and the *Chilicothe,* dwellers in a permanent home. They could put into the field a thousand warriors. Because of their past wanderings

7. "Journal of Captain William Trent," p. 10.

they have been called the "Bedouins of the American Wilderness;" and because of their bravery and heroism in defending their wilderness home against the advance of white invaders they won the proud title of "Spartans of their Race."[8]

"Of all the Indians the Shawnees were the most bloody and terrible, (they) holding all other men, Indians as well as Whites in contempt as warriors in comparison with themselves. This opinion made them more restless and fierce than any other savages; and they boasted that they had killed ten times as many white people, as had any other nation. They were a well formed, active and ingenious people,—were assuming and imperious in the presence of others not of their own nation, and were sometimes very cruel."[9]

The Deleware Nation consisted of five tribal organizations. They like the Shawnees, were one of the parties to the treaty with William Penn in 1682. They once occupied New Jersey and both sides of the Delaware river from which they derived their English name. From here they were driven by the Six Nations, and took refuge in the valley of the Susquehanna, then in that of the Monongahela, and finally, about 1760, in the Ohio Wilderness, where they established themselves in the valleys of the Muskingum and Tuscarawas rivers and their tributaries. Here, in 1770, they had their densest population, though they were really in possession of the eastern half of the present State of Ohio. They had now reached their highest degree of greatness, and could put in the field six hundred and fifty warriors. In history, tradition and fiction, the Delawares have been accorded a high rank among the Indians of North America.[10]

The Wyandot Nation had its chief towns in the valley of the Sandusky river, in what is now Wyandot county; but they were spread out over the whole region from Lake Erie to the Ohio river, with villages along the Hockhocking and other adjacent streams. By the French they were called Hurons, and sometimes Guyandots. They

8. Read Henry Harvey's "History of the Shawnee Indians." The author was long a missionary among them, and records their history as he received it from their wise men.—*V. A. L.*

9. Captain John Stuart's "Memoirs of the Indian Wars and Other Occurrences," p. 49.

10. Read Rev. John Heckewelder's "History, Manners, and Customs of the Indian Nations." Article *Lenni Lenape*, pp. 1-94.

were of the Iroquois linguistic stock.   It was a common saying along
the border that a "Wyandot will not be taken alive."[11]

The tribe of Mingoes of the Ohio Wilderness, was a small organization of the Senecas, one of the Six Nations of New York.   When
first known to the Whites they occupied the Mingo Bottom and all
the region round about the present city of Steubenville in eastern
Ohio; but later gave place to the Delawares, and removed to the upper
waters of the Scioto, where they built their towns on the lands on which
Columbus, the capital city of Ohio now stands.[12]

These Nations of the Ohio Wilderness denied the right of the Six
Nations of New York, to convey to the English a title to the hunting grounds south of the Ohio; and they prepared to defend them
against their White invaders.   They had commingled to some extent
from the beginning of their sojourn in Ohio; and this increased as
their animosities toward each other were supplanted by a common
fear of the enemy of their race.   They gradually grew stronger in
sympathy, and more compact in union as the settlements encroached
upon their forest domain.[13]

The Shawnees and Wyandots realizing that in unity there is
strength, formed an alliance, and in the autumn of 1770, Sir William
Johnson, the British envoy to the Six Nations, learned of a Congress
to be held by the Indians of the Ohio Wilderness, at the Pickaway
Plains—the Shawnee capital—and of this he hastened to write the
Earl of Hillsborough, saying that he had taken measures to be informed, at as early a date as possible, of the proceedings and issues
of the Congress.

To this end he sent Thomas King, an Indian chieftain with an
English name; and An-a-was-ke, next in authority; with Nick-a-roon-
da-se, and several young men.   Johnson awaited their return for
months; then learned that after the Congress completed its work and
adjourned, the Catawbas had escorted his embassadors to Charleston,
South Carolina, where Thomas King sickened and died.   The others
sailed for Philadelphia, but An-a-was-ke died on ship-board; the
others reached their destination, and thence proceeded to Sir William

---

11.   Heckewelder's "Indian Nations," pp. xviii, 95, 119, 130.
12.   "Ohio Archæological and Historical Society Publications," Vol. VI., p. 75.
13.   "History of the Lower Scioto Valley," p. 21.

Johnson's home where Nick-a-roon-da-se, the principal survivor, detailed to him the result of the embassy.   He said that: "Upon Thomas King's arrival at Scioto, he assembled all the nations and first addressed the Shawnees whom he upbraided for returning so far down the Ohio and for confederating with other people unmindful of their engagements * * * The Shawnees answered that the Six Nations had long seemed to neglect them and to disregard the promises they formerly made, of giving them the lands between the Ohio and the Lakes; that thus distressed they went on board their canoes, determined to go whithersoever fortune should drive them, but were stopped many years ago at Scioto by the Six Nations who took them by the hands and fixed them there, charging them to live in peace with the English * * * that they afterward sent belts to strengthen their union with the Six Nations by A-gas-tar-ax, the Seneca chief, and that they never received any answer thereto.   The Shawnees and the representatives of other nations present, then showed some emblematical belts representing themselves and the Illinois Indians in alliance with ten other confederate Nations.[14]

Thus did these western nations, so long the allies and dependents of the Six Nations, now—in that Congress on the banks of the Scioto, in the autumn of 1771,—unite—Shawnees, Delawares, Wyandots, Mingoes, Miamis, Ottawas, Illinois, and others—in a great Northwestern Confederacy, the most powerful that ever menaced the frontiers or confronted English civilization in America.   At its head was placed the famous Shawnee chieftain, Keigh-tugh-qua, signifying the cornstalk, or chief support of his people, and who was therefore known to the Virginians as the Cornstalk Indian.   Thus it was that in the spring of 1774, White men were pressing down from the Alleghenies to the Ohio, and Red men had organized a great Confederacy for the defence of their Country beyond that river.   Each awaited the sound of the tocsin of war.

14. "Documentary History of New York," Vol. II., p. 989.

CHAPTER II.

LORD DUNMORE'S WAR—ITS CAUSES.

FIRST PLAN OF CAMPAIGN—THE OHIO RIVER TO BE THE LINE OF
DEFENSIVE OPERATIONS—SECOND PLAN FOR PROSECUTION OF THE WAR
—EXPEDITION OF MAJOR ANGUS MCDONALD INTO THE OHIO WILDER-
NESS—INSTRUCTIONS TO GENERAL ANDREW LEWIS TO ERECT A FORT AT
THE MOUTH OF THE GREAT KANAWHA RIVER.

"I would find great pleasure in narrating the campaigns under Dunmore and
Lewis, but that would require a volume."—Brantz Mayer's *"Logan and Captain
Michael Cresap,"* p. 58.

"Dunmore's War was a most important event * * * No work with which I
am acquainted does the subject justice. It was truly a great event both in respect
to the parties engaged and the consequences growing out of it; and it has been
passed over too slightly by historians." Drake's *"History and Biography of the
Indians of North America,"* Book V. p. 48.

"It is much to be regretted that a complete history of this campaign has never
been given to the public. Several writers have noticed it incidentally, or given
a meager outline; but no one, it is believed, has entered into these circumstantial
details which alone give interest to such a work."— *Southern Literary Messenger,"*
Vol. XIV., No. 1, p. 18, (1848).

In the year 1774, John Murray, Earl of Dunmore[1] was the Governor of the Colony of Virginia; hence Dunmore's War was a designa-
tion applied to a series of bloody deeds between the Virginians and
the warriors of the Indian confederacy of the Ohio Wilderness, that
year. It stands out conspicuously midway between two great divisions of American History—the Colonial and the Revolutionary Peri-

---

1. John Murray, Fourth Earl of Dunmore, was born in 1732, and was descended
in the female line from the Royal house of Stuart. His ancestors were related
to most of the crowned heads of Europe. (see Sidney Lee's*"Dictionary of Biography"*
Vol. XXXIX., p. 388) the founder of his family being Charles Murray, Master
of Cavalry in the reign of Queen Mary; and who was elevated to the peerage of
Scotland, August 16, 1684, as the First Lord Dunmore. He died in 1710, and
was succeeded by his son John, who inherited his estate and titles and who, as the
Second Earl of Dunmore, became a Representative Peer in 1713, and later a General Officer in the army. He died in April, 1732, and was succeeded in the peerage by his brother William, who became the Third Earl of Dunmore. He wedded
Catherine, his cousin, a daughter of Sir William Murray who afterward became
Lord Neirne; and they had issue John Murray Fourth Earl of Dunmore, our subject. (see Burk's *Peerage of England,"* p. 629). He received a classical education
and was raised to the peerage on the death of his father in 1756. On the 21st
day of February 1759, he was united in marriage with Lady Charlotte Stuart, the
seventh child of Alexander, Sixth Earl of Galloway, a niece of Admiral Sir George
Keith, of the Royal Navy, and a cousin of Lieutenant Richard Fitzgerald of the
Second Life Guards, who fell at Waterloo. In 1761, he took his seat as a representative peer of Scotland in the House of Lords of the Parliament of England
where for nine years, he was associated with the foremost men of Great Britain

JOHN, EARL DUNMORE, VISCOUNT FINCASTLE, BARON MURRAY OF BLAIR, OF MOULIN, AND OF TILLYMOTT.

LAST ROYAL GOVERNOR OF THE COLONY OF VIRGINIA.

(From a painting in the gallery of the State Library at Richmond, Virginia)

ods—but apparently without connection with either. It was the last American war in which American troops waged battle under the flag of England; that is, under the command of a Royal Governor. Its results, as we shall see, wielded a mighty influence upon subsequent history; and there was scarcely a man who was prominent in Western annals in the next forty years who was not in some way connected with it.

A remote cause of the war was the general antagonism of the Red and White races now being brought continually nearer to each other on the boundary between barbarism and civilization along which a tide of emigration broke through the Alleghenies and flowed down in a continuous stream to the Ohio Valley. The immediate causes were the hostilities on the border in the early spring of the year 1774.

Scarcely had the storms of winter subsided when there was an army of surveyors and land-jobbers on the Ohio. In January of this year, William Preston, Surveyor-general, of Fincastle county, which then included all the territory south of the Ohio below the mouth of the Great Kanawha, gave notice to officers and· soldiers who claimed land under his Majesty's proclamation of the 7th of October 1763, and who had obtained warrants for the same from the Earl of Dunmore, to meet his deputy surveyors at the mouth of the Great Kanawha river, on the ensuing 14th of April, that their lands might be located.[2]

When the surveyors—John Floyd and Hancock Taylor—reached that place, they found forty-three men already there. From here a number of them removed twenty miles down the Ohio to the mouth

and was himself a prominent member of that body. (see "Journals of the House of Lords, "Vols. XXX., XXXI., XXXII.) In 1770 he was appointed Governor of New York, but in 1771, became Lieutenant and Governor-General of the Colony of Virginia; and soon therafter arrived at Williamsburg, the Capital of that colony. His Lordship brought with him Captain William Foy, who had served with distinction at the battle of Minden, and subsequently as Lieutenant-Governor of New Hampshire under John Wentworth, to be Secretary of the Colony. The arrival of his family was celebrated with an illumination of the city of Williamsburg and the people with acclamations 'welcomed them to Virginia. When the House of Burgesses met the following May, the capital presented a scene of much gayety, and a Court-Herald published a code of etiquette for the regulation of society of the vice regal court. (see Brock's "Virginia and the Virginians," Vol. I., p. 64) In 1773, Dunmore visited Pittsburg for the purpose of acquiring information regarding the territorial dispute between Virginia and Pennsylvania. In 1774, he commanded the Virginia army of invasion into the Indian country. When the Revolution came, he, like all the colonial Governors in America, adhered to the Royal cause. In 1786, he was appointed Governor of Bermuda Islands, and died at Ramsgate, England, in 1609.

2. Maryland Gazette, March 10th, 1774.

of the Little Guyandotte. Ebenezer Zane, the founder of Wheeling, had a party of surveyors at the mouth of Big Sandy river. George Rogers Clark was with a party numbering ninety at the mouth of the Little Kanawha; and Michael Cresap with another party was at Long Reach, now in Tyler county, West Virginia. The Indians beheld their fate in the occupation, by white men, of their hunting grounds south of the Ohio. They resolved to defend them and hostilities began as early as the first of April that year. Thomas Green, Lawrence Darnell, and William Nash were prospecting for land near the mouth of Lawrence creek, now in Mason county, Kentucky, when they were taken prisoners by a band of Shawnees who held a council over them for three days and then sent them off, telling them, that, henceforth all Virginians found on the Ohio, would be killed. A little later a party of surveyors in Kentucky, nearly opposite the mouth of the Scioto, killed several Shawnee warriors and took thirty horse-loads of skins from them.[3]

An engagement with the Indians occurred near the mouth of the Little Kanawha, and the surveyors there joined Cresap's men and all proceeded up the Ohio to Wheeling. Dr. John Connolly at Fort Dunmore, now Pittsburg,[4] who was Royal Commandant of the "District of West Augusta," addressed a letter to Cresap at Wheeling, apprising him that messengers returned from the Indian nations, stated that a war was enevitable; that the Indians would strike as soon as the season permitted. He urged upon the people of Wheeling to fortify themselves. Cresap received this letter April 21st. A meeting was held on the 26th. Connolly's letter was read, and White men that day voiced a declaration of war against the Indians. Soon it was reported that two Indians and some traders were coming down the river in a canoe and a party from Wheeling ascended the river and killed the Indians. The next day, April 27th, two canoes in which were several Indians, were discovered descending the Ohio, but keeping under cover of Wheeling Island. They were pursued by

---

3. "Washington-Crawford Letters." p. 48.
4. When Lord Dunmore was at Pittsburg in 1773, old Fort Pitt, which had been dismantled after the French and Indian war, in 1763, was falling into decay; but because of the territorial dispute between Virginia and Pennsylvania, and the probability of an Indian war, Dunmore after advising with Dr. John Connolly, thought best to repair the fortress; this was done and the name changed to Fort Dunmore.

Cresap and party to the mouth of Pipe creek, about fifteen miles below Wheeling, where they were overtaken and a battle ensued in which three Indians were killed and scalped and three whites were wounded, one of whom died shortly after. On the West Virginia side of the Ohio, opposite the mouth of Yellow creek, in what is now Grant Magisterial District, Hancock county, West Virginia, lived a man named Joshua Baker, who kept a house of entertainment and sold whiskey. On the lower fork of Yellow creek on the Ohio side, was an Indian encampment in which were a number of relatives of Logan, the celebrated Mingo chieftain; and on April 30th, when a number of these were at the house of Baker, a party of Whites from Short creek, twelve miles above Wheeling, at whose head was Daniel Greathouse, fell upon them and massacred ten in number. This meant all the horrors of an Indian war along the whole frontier. To enter into details would be to prepare a volume.

On the 6th of May, Valentine Crawford, then at Jacob's creek now in Westmoreland county, Pennsylvania, writing Colonel George Washington of the massacre of Logan's people said: "It has almost ruined all the settlements west of the Monongahela. There were more than one thousand people crossed that river going Eastward in a single day."[5]

Two days later, Colonel William Crawford, brother of Valentine, wrote Colonel Washington saying: "Our inhabitants are much alarmed, many hundred having gone Eastward over the Allegheny mountains, and the whole country is vacated as far as the Monongahela."[6] That was in the whole region between that river and the Ohio.

THE HOUSE OF BURGESSES AUTHORIZES GOVERNOR DUNMORE TO PROSECUTE THE WAR AGAINST THE INDIANS:—There was terror along the whole western frontier. Indian atrocities were committed almost daily. Messengers bore tidings of these to Governor Dunmore at Williamsburg, the old Colonial Capital of Virginia. On the 12th of May, Governor Dunmore communicated to the House of Burgesses information which he had received the preceding day con-

---

5. "The Washington-Crawford Letters," p. 85.
6. "The Washington-Crawford Letters," p. 48.

cerning the horrid scenes being enacted on the border.[7] May 13th, that body gave consideration to this as follows:

"It gives us pain, my Lord, to find that the Indians have made frefh encroachments and difturbances on our Frontiers; we have only to requeft that your Excellency will be pleafed to exert thofe powers with which you are fully vefted by the Act of Affembly, for making provifion againft Invafions and Infurrections, which we have no doubt, will be found fufficient to repel the hoftile and perfidious attempts of thofe favage and barbarous Enemies."[8]

In compliance with this action of the House of Burgesses, Lord Dunmore resolved, first, to make the banks of the Ohio the seat of war, or line of defense; or, secondly to invade the Ohio Wilderness, the objective point being the Shawnee Capital on the Pickaway Plains, in the valley of the Scioto river. The military system then in use in the Colony was that embodied in the code prescribed by King George III., at the close of the French and Indian war. It provided that in each county there should be a chief military officer, known as the County-Lieutenant, who should enroll the militia and have general supervision thereof. Below him in rank was a Colonel, then a Lieutenant-Colonel, and lastly a Major. A regiment consisted of five hundred men, or ten companies, of fifty men each, the Company officers being a Captain, Lieutenant, Ensign, and several Sergeants. The Lieutenant and all above him in the county, were known as "Field Officers;" those in the rank below him as "Subalterns." Dunmore determined to give personal direction to the defensive warfare according to this plan. Leaving the Gubernatorial Mansion, July 10th, he crossed the Blue Ridge and established his headquarters at "Greenway Court," the home of Lord Fairfax, in the Lower Shenandoah Valley. On the 5th day of July, Andrew Lewis,[9]

    7. Journal of the House of Burgesses, Session beginning May 5, 1774.
    8. Journal of the House of Burgesses, Session beginning May 5, 1774.
    9. The first extended account of the Lewis family in Virginia was published in 1829, in the *Fincastle* (Va.) *Mirror*, and thence copied into *The Staunton Spectator*. It was written by Hugh Paul Taylor, an employee of the old James River and Kanawha Canal Company, who was fond of dwelling on the old Gælic myths and legends of the British Isles in the third century. From old *Lochlin*, the ancient name of Scandinavia, or of the Peninsula of Jutland, he derived his *Loch Lynn*, which he made the birthplace of Margaret Lynn who became the wife of John Lewis, the emigrant ancestor of the family in Virginia. From the time that Taylor's account was published, the history of the family has contained many contradictions; and he has been followed by Withers, Howe, and others, who enlarged upon these.
    There has been but one member of the family who has written extensively of it. This was George Rockingham Gilmer, a Governor of Georgia, whose mother was a daughter of Thomas Lewis, a niece of General Lewis, and a grand-daughter of

County-Lieutenant of Botetourt county, wrote Governor Dunmore regarding existing conditions in the Greenbrier Valley and New river region. This letter was delivered to him two days after he had gone from Williamsburg on his journey over the Blue Ridge. While stopping at "Rosegill," the home of Ralph Wormsley, one of the Governor's councillors, residing in Middlesex county, he made reply under date of July 12th, to the letter of Lewis. In this he said:—

"I am sorry to find there is so great a probability of your being engaged in a war with the Indians * * * Wait no longer for them to attack you but raise all the men you think willing and able to go down immediately to the mouth of the Great Kanhaway, and there build a Fort and if you think you have force enough that are willing to follow you, proceed directly to their towns and if possible, destroy their towns and magazines; and distress them in every way that is possible. And if you can keep a communication open between you [and] Wheeling Fort (Fort Fincastle) and Fort Dunmore, (at Pittsburg), I am well persuaded [you] will prevent them [the Indians] from crossing the Ohio any more, and consequently from giving any further uneasiness to the inhabitants on that river. I am now on my way up to the Blue Ridge from whence there is already marched a large body of men."[10]

By "the large body of men already marched," Dunmore referred to

John Lewis, the emigrant ancestor. She sat at his elbow while he was writing, and he must have obtained his information regarding the family very largely from her. He says that John Lewis was a native of the county of Dublin, in Ireland; his grand-father, or other more remote ancestor, having removed from Wales to that county during the civil wars in the time of Charles the First: that the Lewellyns of Wales were the kinspeople of the Lewises; that the red hair and irascible temper which still continues to distinguish the family, indicate Welch rather than French, Scotch, or English origin. Continuing, he says that some writers have stated that his wife was of Scotch descent, but circumstances induce him to the opinion that the Lynns emigrated with the Lewises from Wales to Ireland. John Lewis was the first settler on the site of the present city of Staunton, in the Upper Shanandoah Valley, coming thence from Ireland in 1731. At the time of his settlement he had three sons—Thomas, Andrew and William—and two daughters—and to him after his arrival in Virginia, was added his youngest son, Charles. who fell in the battle of Point Pleasant.

Andrew, who commanded at that battle was born in Ireland, in 1720, and wedded Elizabeth Givins of Augusta county, Virginia, and settled at the base of Bent Mountain on the upper Roanoke River, in what became Botetourt county; was long engaged in the Indian wars; served as a Brigadier-General in the Revolution; died, leaving issue, in 1781, and was buried on his estate, "Dropmore", near the present town of Salem, now in Roanoke county, Virginia. There a splendid monument has been erected to his memory. He needs not romance, fiction, nor legend to tell of his exploits. His services in the Border Wars, and in the Revolution, are preserved in the annals of his country. General Lewis was a leading actor in all the events in which he took part; yet fame has trumpeted to the world his exploits with far feebler tone, than the deeds of others of far less importance.

10. Thwaites' "Documentary History of Dunmore's War," p. 86; Original in the Library of the State Historical Society of Wisconsin.

the expedition of Major Angus McDonald[11] to whom he had, before leaving Williamsburg, issued orders similar to those given Lewis, except that he was to erect a fort at the mouth of Wheeling creek on site of the present city of Wheeling. This he hastened to do and with four hundred men collected in the Hampshire hills and Berkeley and Frederick counties, proceeded to Wheeling, where he began the erection of Fort Fincastle (afterward Fort Henry) and was thus engaged until relieved by Captain William Crawford who came from Fort Dunmore (at Pittsburg) with two hundred men, and prosecuted the work to completion; while McDonald with four hundred men— eight companies—prepared for an invasion of the Indian country. Among his Captains were Michael Cresap Sr., Michael Cresap Jr., Hancock Lee, Daniel Morgan, Daniel Cresap ——— Teabaugh, and ——— Hoagland. Leaving Wheeling July 25th, on what was known as the Wakatomica campaign, the army descended the Ohio to the mouth of Fish creek, now in Marshall county, West Virginia. From here the march into the Ohio Wilderness began; Wakatomica, the Shawnee town on the Muskingum river, distant ninety miles away, being the objective point. Jonathan Zane, Thomas Nicholson and Tady Kelly acted as guides. When within six miles of Watacomica, the advance was met by a party of forty or fifty Indians, and a skirmish ensued, in which the Whites had two killed and nine wounded; while of the Indian loss was one killed and several wounded. When the town was reached it was found to be evacuated, the Indians

---

11. MAJOR ANGUS MCDONALD; who commanded the initial or preliminary movement in Dunmore's War, was born on the Highlands of Scotland; he was a grandson of the Lord of Glengary; received a fair education, and was early enlisted in the wars of his time. He was a partisan of the House of Stuart, and took part in the battle of Culloden April 16, 1746. The army was overthrown and after the failure to place the Pretender, Charles Edward, on the throne, young McDonald fled to France where he found refuge with his uncle, Eneas McDonald the grand-father of one of Napolean's field marshals. From there he came to America in 1750, and settled near Winchester, in Frederick county, Virginia, on an estate to which he have the name of "Glengary." Soon afterward he wedded Anna Thompson of Frederick county, in the colony of Maryland and had issue from which has descended a numerous line. He was active in the French and Indian war; was a Vestryman of the old Church in Frederick parish from 1760 to the Revolution. He received a Commission as a Major from Lord Dunmore, a fellow countryman; organized his Battalion; began the erection of Fort Henry at Wheeling; went on the Wakatomica campaign into the Ohio Wilderness; and later marched with Lord Dunmore to the Pickaway Plains. He was made sheriff of Frederick county in 1776—the first under the Commonwealth. Washington appointed him a Lieutenant-Colonel of one of the Virginia regiments, but he was not long to serve his adopted country, for he died at "Glengary" August 19, 1778, aged about seventy years.—From notes compiled by his great grand-son, Marshall McDonald, of Perryville, Virginia.

MAJOR ANGUS McDONALD.

THE BUILDER OF FORT HENRY AT WHEELING, IN 1774, AND COMMANDER OF THE "WAKATOMICA EXPEDITION" OF THAT YEAR.

(From an original painting in the possession of Miss Anne McDonald, of Washington City. Copy supplied by his great-great-granddaughter, Miss Rose McDonald, of Berryville, Virginia.)

lying in ambuscade on the opposite side of the river, believing as they did, that McDonald's men would cross at that place. In this they were disappointed, and sued for peace. They were required to send over five chiefs as hostages; then the army crossed over, only to be told that a treaty could not be made without the presence of the chiefs of the other tribes. These were sent for but did not come; meantime it was discovered that the Indians were removing their old people, women and children and effects to other towns. McDonald having heard of this treachery, laid Wakatomica in ashes; destroyed five hundred bushels of old corn; cut down seventy-five acres of growing corn, and then returned to Wheeling, having with him three chiefs who were sent as hostages to Williamsburg. Immediately thereafter bands of Indians invaded the frontier settlements, spreading terror in all directions. The settlers fled to forts and block-houses but many were either killed or carried into a captivity worse than death.[12]

When Major McDonald and his Valley men returned to the Shenandoah Valley about the 12th of August, they met Governor Dunmore and reported to him the failure of the expedition. His Lordship now abandoned his first plan of campaign, that of making the Ohio river the line of defensive operations—and hastened to put into operation the second—that of the invasion of the Ohio Wilderness. On the 14th of August, he addressed a letter from Frederick county, Virginia, to William Legge, Earl of Dartmouth, English Secretary of State for the American Colonies, in which he said:—

"The Shawnees, Mingoes and some Delawares have fallen on our frontier; killed, scalped, and most cruelly murdered a great many men, women and children. I hope in eight or ten days to march with a body of men over the Allegheny Mountains, and then down the Ohio to the mouth of the Scioto, and if I can possibly fall upon their towns undiscovered, I think I shall be able to put an end to this most cruel war.[13]

Immediately the din of preparation was heard in the Lower Shenandoah Valley. Tents dotted the oak-shaded woodlands around "Greenway Court." James Parsons, Edward Snickers and others traversed the regions round and about for supplies; and the names

12. "American Archives." Fourth series. Vol. I., pp. 722-723.
13. "Documentary History of Dunmore's War," p. 149—Original in the library of the State Historical Society of Wisconsin.

of a thousand men were enrolled on the muster-rolls, among them those who had been with McDonald in the Wakatomica campaign. Two regiments were formed, a first, the "Frederick county Regiment" Colonel William Crawford,[14] commanding; and a second, the "Berkeley county Regiment;" at the head of which was Colonel Adam Stephen;[15] Lord Dunmore was Commander-in-Chief, and the march to the West began. The Berkeley county Regiment left the site of the present city of Winchester August 27th. Dunmore with the Frederick county Regiment followed Braddock's Road, opened seventeen years before, from Winchester, and arrived at the mouth of the South Branch of the Potomac on the 30th of August. Thence onward by way of old Fort Cumberland—now Cumberland City, Maryland—thence over the road constructed for this purpose, by Abraham Hite, Thomas Rutherford and James Wood through the mountains from the Virginia Frontier, to the mouth of Red-stone creek on the Monongahela, where the regiments were separated, the Frederick county men going by way of Fort Dunmore; while the Berkeley men with the beef cattle, crossed the country to Wheeling. At Pitts-

14. William Crawford was born about 1732, in what is now Berkeley county, where in 1749, he became acquainted with young George Washington while the latter was engaged in surveying lands for Lord Fairfax. As an ensign in a Virginia company he was at Braddock's defeat in 1755; the next year was made a Lieutenant, and in 1758 was a Captain in the expedition of General Forbes against Fort Du Quesne. In 1765, he built a cabin at Stuart's Crossing on the Yohogany river, now in Fayette county, Pennsylvania, but then believed to be in Virginia. Here he often entertained George Washington and in 1773 had Lord Dunmore for his guest; his Lordship knew him "to be prudent, active and resolute," hence he was placed at the head of five hundred men in the war of 1774. In 1778 he became Colonel of the Thirteenth Virginia Infantry, known as the "West Augusta Regiment" and was stationed at Pittsburg, the head-quarters of the Western Military Department. In 1782, he commanded the expedition against the Sandusky Indians; was defeated; taken prisoner and burned at the stake, in what is now Wyandotte county, Ohio. The spot of ground on which he perished is now immortal, consecrated as it is, by the blood and martyrdom of this illustrious hero.

15. Adam Stephen who commanded the Berkeley men in Dunmore's War was a native of Pennsylvania, born about 1818, and came to the site of the present city of Martinsburg, West Virginia, about 1738. He enlisted a company for the first Virginia Regiment, in the French and Indian war, which after the death of Joshua Fry, was commanded by Colonel George Washington, with himself as Lieutenant-Colonel; and Andrew Lewis as Major. He was in the engagement at Great Meadows; assisted in building Fort Necessity; and was later in command of Fort Cumberland. He was at Braddock's defeat at the fatal field of Monongahela July 9, 1755; and was with General Forbes at the capture of Fort Du Quesne. At the beginning of the Revolution he became Colonel of a Virginia Regiment; was commissioned a Major-General in 1777. He was in the battles of Trenton, Princeton, and Brandywine, but was dismissed from the service on the charge of intoxication at the battle of Germantown—done so his friends said—to create a place for General Lafayette. He returned to his estate—that on which Martinsburg now stands—and in 1788, was one of the Delegates from Berkeley county to the Virginian Federal Convention which ratified the National Constitution. Thereafter he was long active in civil offices and died in Martinsburg, in 1791, and was buried at that place.

burg, his Lordship was joined by the "West Augusta Battalion" of two hundred men, under the command of Major John Connolly. Valentine Crawford, writing Colonel George Washington from Fort Fincastle, (Wheeling) under date of October 1, 1774, said:—

"I have just time to give you a line or two by Lord Dunmore's Express, to let you know how we go on in this quarter with the Indian war * * * His Lordship arrived here yesterday (September 30th) with about twelve hundred men—seven hundred of whom came by water with his Lordship—and five hundred came under my brother—traveling by land, with the bullocks. His Lordship has sent him with five hundred men— fifty pack-horses and two hundred bullocks to meet Colonel Lewis at the mouth of Hockhocking river below the mouth of the Little Kanawha. His Lordship is to go by water with the rest of the troops in a few days.[16]

In a little time the whole army was at what is now Harris' Ferry in Harris Magisterial District, Wood county, West Virginia, thirteen miles below the city of Parkersburg. Here all crossed the Ohio, swimming the cattle and horses, and on the triangular point of land at the mouth of Hockhocking river on the site of the present town of Hockingport, Ohio, built a stockade fort, which received the name of Fort Gower, in honor of Earl Gower, the personal friend of Dunmore in the British House of Lords. Dunmore's force had been increased by the addition of one hundred men at Wheeling; and at the crossing of the Ohio, he had with him thirteen hundred men; one hundred beeves; two hundred pack-horses; and two hundred and fifty thousand pounds of flour.

16. The "Washington-Crawford Letters," pp. 97-98.

CHAPTER III.

The mustering of an army, by Lord Dunmore, in the northern counties—Frederick, Dunmore, Hampshire and Berkeley—west of the Blue Ridge, and its march to the Ohio, was but half of his second plan of campaign—that of the invasion of the Indian Country. This plan embraced the organization of an army of three thousand men, the Northern Division or Right Wing being commanded by himself; while a Southern Division or Left Wing was to be organized in the Southern counties—Augusta, Botetourt, and Fincastle—west of the Blue Ridge, which should march by another route—the two divisions to be united at some point on the Ohio; whence the march of the entire army into the Ohio Wilderness should begin.

Andrew Lewis was the eldest and most experienced soldier in the Southern counties, and to him, Lord Dunmore issued orders from his head-quarters at "Greenway Court," in Frederick county, under date of July 24th, saying:—

"I desire you to raise a respectable Boddy of men and join me either at the mouth of the grate Kanaway or Whailen (Wheeling) as is most convenient for you.[1] Forward this letter to Colonel William Preston with the greatest Dispatch as I want his assistance, as well as that of your Brother, Charles Lewis. I need not inform you how necessary dispatch is.[2]

At this time Andrew Lewis,[3] was County-Lieutenant of Botetourt county, his home being at "Dropmore," at the base of Bent Mountain near the present town of Salem, now in Roanoke county; and

---

1. The reader will observe that Dunmore here named two points on the Ohio for the uniting of the two divisions. but left it to General Lewis to decide which of these it should be—Wheeling or the mouth of the Great Kanawha.
2. "Documentary History of Dunmore's War." p. 98. Original in the library of the State Historical Society of Wisconsin.
3. There was no promotion for Andrew Lewis. In the military establishment of the Colony, he retained the title of Colonel, but because he discharged the duties of a Brigadier General in this war, and held that rank in the Revolutionary war, he is always spoken of as General Lewis, and therefore thus disignated in this work.—V. A. L.

William Fleming[4] the Colonel of the county, resided at "Belmont" then in Botetourt, but now in Montgomery county; and William Preston was County-Lieutenant and Surveyor-General of Fincastle county, his home being at "Smithfield," now Blacksburg, in Montgomery county; and William Christian[5] Colonel of the county, lived on "Dunkard's Bottom" on the west side of New river, now in Pulaski county. Charles Lewis was County-Lieutenant of Augusta county, his home being near the present village of Williamsville, on Cowpasture river, then in Augusta, but now in Bath county.

Promptly on receipt of these orders from Dunmore, General Lewis sent copies thereof to all the military officers of the Southern Counties; and at the same time summoned them to attend a council of war at his home, on the 12th of August. In this call he said:— "Don't faile to come; and let us do something. I would, as matters stand, run great risk rather than a miscarriage should happen." At this council, plans were completed for enlisting the troops; and it was determined that all should rendezvous at "Camp Union" so designated because the troops were to be united there, on the Savannah or Big Levels about seven miles from White Sulphur Springs, on the site of the present town of Lewisburg, the seat of Justice of Greenbrier

4. Colonel William Fleming was born at Jedburg, Scotland, February 18, 1729, and was the son of the sixth Lord Sterling, Earl of Wigton. He received a thorough education; was graduated in medicine from the University of Edinburgh; and entered the British navy as Assistant Surgeon. A fellow-countryman—Robert Dinwiddie—was Governor of the Colony of Virginia in 1755, and he resolved to come hither. This he did, and the same year received a Commission as Ensign, in Washington's Regiment, in which he served until the close of the French and Indian war. In 1762, he served as Lieutenant under Major Andrew Lewis at Fort Chiswell, and the same year became a Captain in the Berkeley—Hampshire Regiment, commanded by Colonel Adam Stephen. In 1774, he was residing at his home—"Belmont," in Botetourt county, and commanded the regiment, mustered there, at the battle of Point Pleasant. He was a member of the First senate of the Commonwealth of Virginia; in 1780, he became a member of the Council of State, and in June of that year, he was the Acting Governor of the Commonwealth. Colonel Fleming died at "Belmont" August 1795, and carried to his grave, in his body, a bullet received at the battle of Point Pleasant, twenty-one years before.

5. Colonel William Christian was a representative of a family which long resided on the Isle of Man. Gilbert Christian wedded Margaret Richardson in Ireland, and their children, one of whom was Israel, came to Virginia, and settled on Christian's creek, in Augusta county, in 1733. Here William, the subject," was born in 1743. He was a member of the House of Burgesses from Fincastle county in 1774, and was Colonel of his county at the time of Dunmore's war. In 1775 he was a member of the Virginia Convention that assembled March 20th, and same year he became Lieutenant-Colonel of the First Virginia Regiment of which Patrick Henry was Colonel. In 1776, he became Colonel of the first battalion of Virginia and commander of an expedition against the Cherokee Indians. In 1780, he commanded another expedition against that nation; and was the next year, appointed by General Green, head of a Commission to conclude a treaty with them. In 1785, he removed to Kentucky and settled near Louisville. The year following, he with others, pursued a party of Indians across the Ohio, where he was shot and killed on the site of Jeffersonville, Indiana.

County, West Virginia. All were to be there in readiness to march to the Ohio on the 30th of August. Immediately the din of preparation was heard throughout the Southern counties. Colonel Charles Lewis established his headquarters at Staunton; Colonel William Christian fixed his at the "New River Ford," later known as Ingles' Ferry; Colonel William Fleming made his at his home at "Belmont." General Lewis and Colonel William Christian moved here, there, and everywhere, encouraging enlistments, and looking after supplies. Recruiting stations were established at Warm Springs, now Bath county; at other points in the valley of the Cowpasture and Bullpasture rivers; at Staunton and other points on the upper tributaries of the Shenandoah river; at Tinkling Springs and elsewhere in Southern Augusta; at Smithfield, "Belmont," the "New River Ford" and elsewhere in Botetourt; and at "Royal Oak," "Castle Woods," "Seven Mile Ford," on Holston river, at Wolf Hills, (now Abingdon); at "King's Meadows" on the site of the present city of Bristol, Tennessee-Virginia, and other places in Fincastle.

One company did not wait for another, but as speedily as organized, repaired to Camp Union, the place of general rendezvous. Captain John Stuart's company of Greenbrier Valley men arrived August 1st—the first at Camp Union. Then came Captain John Dickinson's company from the valley of the Cowpasture and Jackson's rivers; Captains Alexander McClennahan and George Mathews arrived with their companies from Staunton; the company of Captain Andrew Lockridge came from Bullpasture river, now in Highland county; Captain John Lewis (son of Thomas) and Captain Benjamin Harrison reported with their companies from that part of Augusta, now included in Rockingham county; Captains George Moffatt and Samuel McDowell came with their companies from Southern Augusta—that part now included in Rockbridge county. The Fincastle Battalion was recuited mainly in the valleys of the Holston, Clinch, Watauga, and Powell's rivers. Captain Evan Shelby brought with him fifty-two of the first settlers from the valley of Watauga, chiefly from what is now Sullivan and Carter counties, Tennessee; the companies of Captains William Russell, William Campbell, William Herbert, and John Floyd were from the valleys of the Clinch and Holston river settlements; and Captains Anthony Bledsoe and Joseph Crockett came from along the southern banks of the upper New river. These companies assembled at the "New River Ford," latter "Ingles' Ferry," and thence proceeded down that river and through Rich Creek Gap, now "Symms' Gap," in Peters' Mountain; thence across the present county of Monroe, West Virginia to Camp Union. Colonel John Field, (acting Captain) brought a company of Culpeper county Minute Men; Captain Thomas Slaughter came with a company from Dunmore, (now Shenandoah county;) and Captain Thomas Buford arrived with a company of Riflemen from Bedford county. Later still, eighty unorganized men came from Augusta county; and a like number from Culpeper; and Captain James Harrod brought out of the Kentucky wilderness the founders of Harrodsburg, the oldest town in that State.

Colonel Charles Lewis executed his will at Staunton, August 10th, and then hastened away to Camp Union. Colonel Fleming arrived there on the 29th of August; General Andrew Lewis came on the 1st of September; and Colonel William Christian, on the 6th of that month. Colonel William Preston did not accompany the army because of sickness in his family.

The complete organization of the army as perfected at Camp Union may be shown as follows:—

SOUTHERN DIVISION OR LEFT WING OF LORD DUNMORE'S ARMY.

General Andrew Lewis, Commanding.

THE AUGUSTA COUNTY REGIMENT.

Colonel Charles Lewis, Commanding.

CAPTAINS OF COMPANIES.

Captain John Dickinson.	Captain Samuel McDowell.
Captain George Moffatt.	Captain Alexander McClennahan.
Captain George Mathews.	Captain Andrew Lockridge.
Captain John Skidmore.	Captain Samuel Wilson.
Captain John Lewis.	Captain Benjamin Harrison.
Captain William Nalle.	

THE BOTETOURT COUNTY REGIMENT.

Colonel William Fleming, Commanding. (450 men)

CAPTAINS OF COMPANIES.

Captain Philip Love.

Captain John Lewis.

Captain John Stuart.

Captain James Ward.

Captain Mathew Arbuckle.

Captain John Murray.

Captain Robert McClennahan.

Captain Henry Pauling.

THE FINCASTLE COUNTY BATTALLION.

Colonel William Christian, Commanding. (350 men)

CAPTAINS OF COMPANIES.

Captain William Russell.

Captain Joseph Crockett.

Captain William Campbell.

Captain Anthony Bledsoe.

Captain Evan Shelby.

Captain William Herbert.

Captain John Floyd.

INDEPENDENT COMPANIES.

The Culpeper Minute Men, Colonel John Field, commanding (40 men); The Dunmore County Volunteers, Captain Thomas Slaughter, commanding, (40 men); the Bedford County Riflemen, Captain Thomas Buford, commanding. (44 men); the Kentucky Pioneers, Captain James Harrod, commanding. (27 men.)

The Culpeper Minute Men were attached to the Augusta Regiment; the Bedford Riflemen to the Botetourt Regiment; and the Dunmore Volunteers, and the Kentucky Pioneers to the Fincastle Battalion.

Colonel William Fleming and Captains Thomas Buford and Robert McClennahan, all regularly educated physicians, composed the Medical Board of the army. Rev. ———— Terry was Chaplain of the army. Major Thomas Posey was chief Commissary and Quarter Master-General; Sampson Mathews was Quarter-Master of the Augusta Regiment with John Lyle as his assistant; Thomas Ingles was Quarter-Master of the Botetourt Regiment; and Anthony Bledsoe was Commisssary of the Fincastle Battalion. James Hughes was Pack-horse Master; William McClure chief Driver of Cattle; John Warwick was chief Butcher; Captain Mathew Arbuckle was chief Guide; Frederick Burley was chief Indian Spy; and John Coalter, carpenter. The lead used, came from the mines at Fort Chiswell, on the Upper New river, then the seat of Justice of Fincastle county; and the powder was largely manufactured near the Natural Bridge, now in Rockbridge county. The cattle were from the southern counties west of the Blue Ridge, and the flour was ground on water-mills in the Shenandoah Valley.

This army at Camp Union was the most remarkable body of men that had ever assembled on the American frontier. Of the men comprising it, some had been with Washington at the surrender of Fort Necessity; some with Braddock at the fatal field of Monongahela; others with Forbes at the capture of Fort Du Quesne; and still others with Boquet in the Ohio Wilderness; and all, or nearly all, had been engaged all their lives in the Border wars. Hence the men collected at Camp Union were not only schooled in both the English and Colonial military systems, but were familiar with the methods of Indian warfare as well. Every man knew his duty and the importance of the undertaking in which he was engaged. "It may be doubted if a braver or physically finer set of men will ever get together on this continent.⁶

This army was not uniformed as such; a few of the officers on Colonial establishment, wore the regular military uniform, but far the greater number wore the individual costume of the Border. They were clad in the hunting-shirt with leather leggings; breeches of domestic make; and caps made from the skins of wild animals or knit from wool. Each carried the long flint-lock rifle, or English musket, with bullet-pouches and quaintly carved powder-horns; with tomahawk and butcher knife. They had been the Border Rangers of past years, but now an offensive warfare was theirs. It was an army composed of fighters impatient for the fray. It was an army of civilized men, encamped on the borderland of a Savage Empire. There on the "Levels" around Camp Union were heard the voices of men, the neighing of horses, the lowing of cattle, the rattle of the drums, and the sharp whistle of the fife—sounds all so strange in the solitude of the Allegheny wilderness.

---

6. Roosevelt's "Winning of the West," Vol. I., p. 222.

CHAPTER IV.

THE WESTWARD MARCH OF GENERAL ANDREW LEWIS' ARMY FROM CAMP UNION TO THE OHIO RIVER.

THE ARMY LEAVING CAMP UNION—THE ADVANCE THROUGH THE MOUNTAINS
TO THE GREAT KANAWHA RIVER—THENCE DOWN THAT RIVER TO
CAMP POINT PLEASANT ON THE OHIO RIVER.

As usual some were behind and the army was not ready to move from Camp Union the first of September, as provided by the council of war, held at the home of General Lewis on the 12th of the preceeding August. On Tuesday, the 30th of August, Lord Dunmore, then at the mouth of the South Branch of the Potomac on his westward march to the Ohio, wrote General Lewis, expressing his Lordship's warmest wishes, and that he (General Lewis) would with all his troops, join him at the mouth of the Little Kanawha river— now Parkersburg,[1] West Virginia. Lewis received this letter on Sunday, September 5th, ensuing, and made reply by saying that it was then too late to alter the route to the Ohio, and he must needs proceed to the mouth of the Great Kanawha.[2]

ADVANCE OF THE AUGUSTA REGIMENT:—On Tuesday, September 6th, there was a busy scene at Camp Union. The cattle were being corralled, the pack-horses laden; then the drums and fifes were heard and the Augusta Regiment, together with Colonel Stuart's company of the Botetourt Regiment, fell into line, and with its drove of cattle and cavalcade of pack-horses, passed over the high hill west of Camp Union and disapeared in the wilderness. We know but little of its march through the Alleghenies, one hundred and three miles to the

---

1. It will be observed that Lord Dunmore desired General Lewis to meet him at the mouth of the Little Kanawha instead of the Great Kanawha. After conversing with Major McDonald and others familiar with the geography of the Ohio Valley, he had learned that the route to the Pickaway Plains by way of the Valley of the Hockhocking river was much shorter than to descend the Ohio to the mouth of the Great Kanawha and then go hence.—V. A. L.

2. "Documentary History of Dunmore's War," p. 190. Original in the library of the State Historical Society of Wisconsin.

mouth of the Elk river, on the Great Kanawha—now Charleston the capital of West Virginia. Colonel William Christian writing Colonel William Preston the next day, says:—

"Colonel Charles Lewis marched yesterday with about 600 Augusta men. His business is to proceed as far as the mouth of Elk, then to make canoes to take down the flour. He took with him 108 beeves and 500 pack-horses carrying 54,000 pounds of flour."[3]

This left a shortage of beef at Camp Union but Sampson Mathews, the Quarter-Master of the Augusta Regiment was expected to furnish an immediate supply. His contract was to furnish 160,000 pounds of flour, of which 80,000 had been delivered; of this 54,000 had gone forward with the Augusta Regiment. Caleb Atwater, an early historian of the State of Ohio, when speaking of this march said:—

"His route lay wholly through a trackless forest. All his baggage, his provisions, and even his ammunition, had to be transported on pack-horses, that were clambering about among the tall cliffs, or winding their way through dangerous defiles, ascending or descending the lofty summits of the Alleghanies. The country at this time, in its aspect is one of the most romantic and wild in the whole Union. Its natural features are majestic and grand. Among these lofty summits and deep ravines, nature operates on a scale of grandeur, simplicity and sublimity, scarcely ever equaled in any other region, and never surpassed in the world. * * * During nineteen entire days, this gallant band pressed forward descending from the heights of the Alleghany mountains, to the mouth of the Kenhawa, a distance of one hundred and sixty miles."[4]

The second body of troops to leave Camp Union was the Culpeper Minute men—forty in number—under Colonel John Field, (then serving as captain) who brought orders from Lord Dunmore, to General Lewis to admit him and the Culpeper men to service in the Southern Division. Field followed in the wake of the Augusta Regiment, gone thirty hours before, but the smaller body moved the more rapidly, and came up with the advance on the third day.[5]

ADVANCE OF THE BOTETOURT REGIMENT:—Captain Philip Love, writing Colonel William Preston on September 12th, says:—"The

---

3. "Documentary History of Dunmore's War." p. 185. Original in the library State Historical Society of Wisconsin.
4. "Atwater's History of the State of Ohio." Second Edition, p. 112.
5. Letter of Colonel Christian to Colonel Preston, dated "Camp Union," September 7th, 1774; printed in "Documentary History of Dunmore's war." p. 185.

Botetourt troops marches in a few hours for the mouth of Elk, our next post from this."[6]

Colonel William Christian writing Colonel William Preston says:—

"General Lewis' has just marched with Colonel Fleming and the Botetourt troops, (men from his own county) with an addition of the companies of Captains Shelby and Russell, from Fincastle, and Buford's Bedford County Riflemen."

We do not know how many pack-horses or beeves went forward with Colonel Fleming's Regiment. It took with it 18,000 pounds of flour from Camp Union, leaving 8,000 pounds at that place. Major Christian was left in command with the remainder of the Fincastle troops, the Dunmore Volunteers, and a few men from each of the counties of Augusta and Culpeper. Several persons were absent collecting supplies. Already 72,000 pounds of flour had gone forward and Christian was expecting 130 horse-loads to arrive the next day. He had information that there were 96 horse-loads at the Warm spring, now in Bath county; and that there were from 30,000 to 40,000 pounds to be brought up from beyond these Springs.[8]

JOURNAL AND ORDERLY BOOK OF COLONEL FLEMING.

Fortunately the Journal and Orderly Book[9] kept by Colonel William Fleming has been preserved, and from these we learn of the westward march of the Botetourt Regiment, and the Fincastle companies and Buford's Riflemen which accompanied it.

From it we make extracts and insert material relating to the region through which the march was performed—that from Camp Union, to "Camp Point Pleasant"—a distance of one hundred and sixty miles.

September 11th, Sunday—The last day for the Botetourt Regiment at Camp Union;; Parole[10] Greenbrier. There was a stirring scene at that place. The second Regiment with companies attached thereto were to

6. "Documentary History of Dunmore's War," p. 195. Original in the library of the State Historical Society of Wisconsin.
7. "Documentary History of Dunmore's War." p. 196. Original in the library of the State Historical Society of Wisconsin.
8. "Documentary History of Dunmore's War." Original in the library of the State Historical Society of Wisconsin.
9. The original is in the library of the State Historical Society of Wisconsin. It is printed in the "Documentary History of Dunmore's War," pp. 313-360.
10. The parole was a watchword or password issued by the commanding Officer to officers of the guard. It differed from the countersign, which was a word given to all guards. It was usually at that time, a geographical term but sometimes the name of an individual.

move for the West. Six days had elapsed since the Augusta Regiment departed from Camp Union. Posey and Ingles were having the pack-horses laden and the Quarter-Master was arranging for the transporation of tools and ammunition.

September 12th, *Monday*—Divine service at 12 o'clock M. Marched from Camp Union; crossed Muddy Creek Mountain, and encamped at "Camp Pleasants," seen miles west of Camp Union; Parole *Frederick*. First Camp: Now near Asbury Post Office in Blue Sulphur Magisterial District, Greenbrier county, West Virginia.

September 13th, *Tuesday*—Resumed the March; passed "Hamilton's Plantation" and "Jackson's Clearing," and having marched eleven miles, encamped on a branch of Muddy Creek—"a bad place for both food and good water;" Parole *George*. Second camp: Now near Elton Post Office in Green Sulphur Magisterial District, Summers county.

September 14th, *Wednesday*—Marched up a branch one and one half miles and then passed over to Meadow Creek, a tributary of Gauley river; over Walker's creek, a tributary of New river, where the army encamped; Parole *Quebec*. Third Camp: Now near Backus Post Office, in Quinni-mont Magisterial District, Fayette county.

September 15th, *Thursday*—Left the third camp and marched up Buffalo Spring Lick, and fell in on the road made by the advance, under Colonel Charles Lewis, which was followed for a mile and a half. Then another mile and a half, to the fourth encampment on Buffalo Fork, a western affluent of Meadow river. Manuscript torn. Fourth Camp: Now near Crickmer Post Office still in Quinnimont Magisterial District, Fay-ette county.

September 16th, *Friday*—March resumed. Firing of guns forbidden. Here on this day they were joined by Captain Robert McClennahan's and Captain Henry Pauling's companies, which were left behind to bring up some beef cattle which were lost. Parole *Washington*. Fifth camp: Now in the vicinity of Maplewood Post Office, Sewell Mountain Magisterial District, Fayette county.

September 17th, *Saturday*—Left the fifth encampment at an early hour, and took up the line of march westward. The march was over "Chestnut Hills;" crossed Great and Little Laurel creeks, the first of which empties into the New river near Quinnimont, at what is known as the "Warrior's Ford," and passed Mann's Hunting Camp on a stream now known as Mann's creek, an eastern branch of New river. Parole

Byrd. Sixth camp: Now near Winona Post Office, in Nuttall Magistrial District, Fayette county.

September 18th, *Sunday*—Started early in the morning and marched twelve miles over broken ridges covered with a chestnut forest and late at night encamped on Laurel Run. Parole *Corbin.* Seventh camp: Now near Mountain Cove Post Office, on Shade creek, a tributary of Mill creek, in Mountain Cove Magisterial District, Fayette county.

September 19th, *Monday*—The line of march was taken up. It was a day of alternate showers and sunshine; early in the day the present site of Ansted, in Fayette county, was reached and then began the ascent of Gauley mountain by a different path from that of Lewis' Advance Column, over the crest of which the columns passed, and thence down to the head of Rich Creek, a southern tributary of Gauley River. But six miles were made and an encampment fixed at the head of Rich Creek. Parole *Page.* Eighth camp: Still in Mountain Cove Magisterial District, Fayette county.

September 20th, *Tuesday*—There was an inspection of arms by the Captains, and then the march began and continued down Rich Creek for five miles, crossing it many times until the Gauley River was reached. This was "about one hundred yards wide, a stony ugly fording." This river was crossed by two fords within one and a half miles of Rich Creek, and encamped on Bell Creek, having marched eleven miles. Parole *Johnson.* Ninth camp: Now on Bell creek in Falls Magisterial District, Fayette county.

September 21st. *Wednesday*—The army proceeded up Lick (Bell) Creek five miles, passed the divide, and over on the head of Kelly's creek, "thick with laurel for two miles" then the western tops became lower, the valley to widen, the tulip,[11] maple, pawpaw, with leatherwood, and peavine, and buffalo grass made their appearance; then appeared the sweet gum; and then the Great Kanawha river, two hundred yards wide, made its appearance. It was the site of the settlement of Walter Kelly, who was killed by the Indians two years before. Thence the march continued down

---

11. "Leaving home in August, they (the men of the Southern Division), joined the army of western Virginia at Camp Union, on the Great levels of Greenbrier. From that place, now called Lewisburg, to the mouth of the Great Kanawha, the distance is about one hundred and sixty miles. At that time there was not even a trace over the rugged mountains; but the young woodsmen who formed the advance party moved expeditiously with their pack-horses and droves of cattle through the home of the wolf, the deer, and the panther. After a fortnight's struggle, they left behind them the last rocky masses of the hill-tops; and, passing between the gigantic growth of primeval forests, in which at that season the golden hue of the linden, the sugar tree, and the hickory contrasted with the glistening green of the laurel, the crimson of the sumach, and the shadows of the sombre hemlock, they descended to the widening valley of Elk River."—Bancroft's "History of the United States," Vol. IV., p. 86.

to an encampment opposite the mouth of Cabin Creek. Parole *Kanhaway*. Tenth camp: Now opposite the mouth of Cabin Creek, in Cabin Creek Magisterial District, Kanawha county.

September 22d, *Thursday*—March continued down the north side of the river. Arrived at the mouth of Elk river, the present site of Charleston, the capital of West Virginia, where it joined the Augusta Regiment. Eleevnth camp. Parole *Charlestown*. Distance by computation from Camp Union, one hundred and eight miles. The actual distance was one hundred and three miles. Both regiments engaged in building a store-house and making canoes for transporting supplies down the Great Kanawha.

September 23rd, *Friday*—Details of men made to work on the canoes and the scouts reported early for instructions. All the tools in camp were put in working order. Parole *Dunkirk*.

September 24th, *Saturday*—Pack-horses were sent back to Camp Union for flour. The men detailed for this purpose were busy with the canoes. A court martial consisting of Colonel Fleming, President, and five Captains, sat to try Timothy Fitzpatrick for stealing a gun. He was acquitted and joined Captain McDowell's company. The provisions and ammunition were deposited in a magazine, built for the purpose. Three scouts were sent up Elk river toward Pocatalico; three across the Kanawha to Coal river; and some down the Kanawha on the north side. Divine services were held at twelve o'clock. Parole *Bedford*.

September 25th, *Sunday*—James Mooney, one of the scouts sent over Kanawha to Coal river returned and reported that four miles below the mouth of Elk, they had discovered the tracks of three horses, one shod, and two moccasin tracks that had passed them in the night going down the river. All attended divine services and had a good discourse. Scouts sent to the mouth of the Kanawha, launched their canoes at the mouth of Elk, and began the voyage down the river. Parole *Winchester*.

September 26th, *Monday*—Men at work were exempted from guard duty. Orders prohibiting the miscellaneous firing of guns were read at the head of each company immediately after the beating of Reveille. Parole *Cumberland*.

September 27th, *Tuesday*—At a review of the Botetourt Regiment including the Fincastle and Culpeper men attached thereto, there were 523 men in line, and together with the Augusta Regiment, 1000 answered roll-call, that meaning exclusive of the sick and those on service or command in this vicinity. Parole *Duke*.

September 28th, *Wednesday*—Scouts from Coal River returned and reported that they had discovered where fifteen Indians had encamped. Captain Arbuckle with his scouts, was ordered out after them, but failed to come up with them. The confusion in camp resulting from the sale of liquors by the sutlers, made it necessary to prohibit the sale otherwise than on the orders of the Captains; and no more than the present stock was to be brought into Camp. Parole *Prince*.

September 29th, *Thursday*—James Fowler returned. He was one of the scouts which left on the 25th for the mouth of the Great Kanawha. He reported that when they were within fifteen miles of the mouth of the river, they saw two fires on its banks; that on their making a noise these were covered up; that on his return up the river in the canoe he saw five Indians with three horses going down the river. Parole *Westmoreland*.

September 30th, *Friday*—Drums beat at day break; the fleet of canoes —27 in number—which had been constructed, were taken one and a half miles up Elk river, where it was a hundred yards wide and where there was a "fording." The cattle and pack-horses were driven over, and there the army crossed the river and encamped on the level plain below the mouth of the Elk. It was "still dead running water." Parole *King*. Twelfth camp: Now on the present site of West Charleston, in Charleston Magisterial District, Kanawha county.

THE MARCH OF LEWIS' ARMY FROM THE MOUTH OF ELK RIVER TO THE MOUTH OF THE GREAT KANAWHA.

October 1st, *Saturday*—Because of incessant rain the army remained in camp throughout the day and ensuing night. Parole *Pitt*. Same camp as on September 30th.

October 2d, *Sunday*—Early in the morning the army formed for line of march down the north side of the Great Kanawha river; Captain Lewis of the Botetourt Line led the advance. That line was the left column, while the Augusta Line was the right; both flanks were covered by one hundred men each. In the center were the beef cattle and pack-horses. The orders to march were given, and the army made twelve miles that day. Parole *Burk*. Thirteenth camp: now in Union Magisterial District, opposite the mouth of Coal River—now St. Albans, Kanawha county.

October 3rd, *Monday*—The march was continued, and in the afternoon Pocatalico river crossed and an encampment affected one mile below the mouth of that stream, the distance from the last camp being eight miles. Parole *Dinwiddie*. Fourteenth camp: Now in Pocatalico Magisterial District, Putnam county.

October 4th, *Tuesday*—Onward marched the army through the wilderness and through the narrows at Red House Shoals "where large masses of rock the height of which exceeded the base, stood partly much in line;" they saw the "Fallen Timber" where the hills were swept "bare as a field," and encamped two miles below the mouth of Hurricane creek. Parole *Fauquier*. Fifteenth camp: now near Midway Post Office, in Union Magisterial District, Putnam county.

October 5th, *Wednesday*—The march was resumed early in the morning; Buffalo Creek was crossed; the site of the present town of Buffalo passed; Eighteen-Mile creek forded; the site of Leon passed and an encampment made two miles below the mouth of Thirteen-Mile creek, the distance from the last encampment being twelve miles. Parole *Charlestown*. Sixteenth camp: Encampment on the Yauger farm, Cologne Magisterial District, Mason county.

October 6th, *Thursday*—Again the march continued; early in the morning Ten-mile creek was crossed; Upper and Lower Debby creeks passed; then Eight-mile and Three-mile creeks forded and late in the afternoon the army crossed Crooked creek and encampd on th upper trangular point of land at the confluence of the Great Kanawha and Ohio rivers, having marched eleven miles. It was a magnificent scene. The dense forest clothed in its autumnal tints; and the rivers at low-water, with the Ohio resembling a lake and the Great Kanawha an estuary, the whole landscape presenting an enchanting scene. An army of weary men appreciated it, and bestowed upon it the name of *Camp Point Pleasant*. Parole *York*. "Encamped in the forks of the river" says Major Ingles, "in safe possession of a fine Encampment, we thought ourselves a terror to all the Indian tribes on the Ohio."[12]

The accuracy with which Colonel Fleming estimated distances in surprising. These he gives for each day's march down the Great Kanawha, from the mouth of Elk, to the Ohio, equals fifty-seven and three-fourth miles; and the actual distance between these two points by railroad measurements is fifty-seven miles.

The fourth detachment to leave Camp Union, was the company of Captain William Herbert, of the Fincastle Battalion, which took up the line of march therefrom on Friday, September 23rd. When

---

12. "Documentary History of Dunmore's War," p. 258. Original in the library of the State Historical Society of Wisconsin.

it came up with the regiments in advance does not appear; but this was doubtless at the mouth of Elk river about the first of October.

DEPARTURE OF THE FINCASTLE BATTALION FROM CAMP UNION:— Colonel Christian left Camp Union for the west, Tuesday, September 27th, having with him the companies of Captains William Campbell, Joseph Crockett, George Moffatt and John Floyd, of the Fincastle Battalion; Captain Thomas Slaughter with the Dunmore Volunteers; Captain James Harrod with the Kentucky Pioneers; about eighty unorganized Minute Men from Culpeper county, who arrived too late to march with Colonel Field; and a like number who came from Augusta county, after the regiment therefrom, had marched from Camp Union. He estimated the total number at about 400 men.

We know little of the march of Christian through the mountains, save that it was made in shorter time that that of either of the divisions gone before. He arrived at the mouth of Elk river—now Charleston—on the 6th of October, eight days after leaving Camp Union, the distance being one hundred and three miles. October 7th, General Lewis at the mouth of the Great Kanawha, received letters from Christian stating that he was at the mouth of Elk "with 220 men, with 350 beeves; 24,000 lbs. of flour, and a supply of gunpowder." Sergeant Obediah Trent, of Captain Pauling's company, with a party of canoe-men, was sent up the Kanawha to bring down supplies.[13] On the 8th, Christian having detailed Captain Slaughter with the Dunmore Volunteers, to remain at the mouth of Elk, he, with the remainder, crossed that river and began the march down the north side of the Great Kanawha. The night was spent in the vicinity of what is now the West Virginia Colored Institute, in Union Magisterial District, Kanawha county. On the 9th, when Christian was near what is now Red House Shoals, on the Great Kanawha, he was met by scouts with a letter to him from General Lewis, requesting him to leave fifty beeves at Elk for those who should be there from time to time. This Christian could not do for he was then too far on his march.[14] The march was therefore continued and

---

13. "Documentary History of Dunmore's War," p. 340. Original in the library of the State Historical Society of Wisconsin.
14. "Documentary History of Dunmore's War," p. 267.

that evening an encampment was made near where the town of Buffalo, in Buffalo Magisterial District, Putnam county, now stands.

THE DETACHMENT LEFT AT CAMP UNION:—Colonel Christian left Captain Anthony Bledsoe of the Fincastle Battalion in command at Camp Union. The troops with him were those of his own company, and the sick of the entire army who had been unable to leave with their respective commands. He was to receive and forward the supples collected when the pack-horses were returned from the mouth of Elk. A number of these returned September 30th, but in such a jaded condition that they must rest before going to Warm Springs for their loads of flour. There was at that place 150 horse-loads, and an equal number at Staunton.[15] Under date of Saturday, October 15th, he again wrote Colonel Preston from Camp Union saying:—

"I propose starting from this place tomorrow with about two hundred horses and eighty cattle and hope to reach the mouth of New River (Great Kanawha) in 12 days, if the weather is good."[16]

Because of stirring news from the front he never marched on the expedition.

---

15. "Documentary History of Dunmore's War," p. 223. Original in the library of the State Historical Society of Wisconsin.
16. "Documentary History of Dunmore's War," p. 261. Original in the library of the State Historical Society of Wisconsin.

CHAPTER V.

THE BATTLE OF POINT PLEASANT.

The battle of Point Pleasant was fought exactly three months from the day that Lord Dunmore left the gubernatorial mansion at Williamsburg; and in that brief time an army numbering more than twenty-seven hundred men had been organized in two divisions, each composed almost exclusively of frontiersmen west of the Blue Ridge and placed in the Ohio Valley. On Sunday, the ninth of October, the Northern Division or right wing, comprising the Berkeley and the Frederick County Regiments, and the West Augusta Battalion, the whole numbering thirteen hundred men, and commanded by Lord Dunmore in person, lay at Fort Gower, on the northwest bank of the Ohio, at the mouth of the Hockhocking river, now in Athens county, Ohio. The Southern Division or left wing, composed of the Augusta and the Botetourt Regiments; and the companies of Shelby, Russell, and Herbert, of the Fincastle Battalion; together with Buford's Bedford county Riflemen, the whole commanded by General Andrew Lewis, lay at Camp Point Pleasant, at the mouth of the Great Kanawha river. Colonel Christian with the companies of Campbell, Crockett and Floyd, of the Fincastle Battalion, and Harrod's Kentucky Pioneers, together with a number of unorganized men from the counties of Augusta and Culpeper, lay on the north or right bank of the Great Kanawha river, distant about twenty-five miles from its mouth. Captain Thomas Slaughter with the Dunmore Volunteers was at the mouth of Elk river—on the site of the Capital city of West Virginia—and Captain Anthony Bledsoe, with his company of Fincastle troops was still at Camp Union, on the Big Levels of Greenbrier. Christian's men were the only ones that moved that day; this was due to his desire to come up with General Lewis before he would cross the Ohio. At Camp Point Pleasant a communication had been received from Lord Dunmore stating that he should move directly across the country from Fort Gower to the Pickaway Plains,

and requesting Lewis to join him at the latter place. Preparations were
made to resume the march for this purpose.   Then, says Major
Ingles[1]: "After hearing a good sermon preached by the Rev.
Mr. Terry, (we) went to repose." That evening General Lewis'
scouts reported to him that there was so no enemy within fifteen miles
of the camp. But fleet-footed Indian warriors from the peaks of the
Alleghenies, and the highlands along the Great Kanawha, had watched
the progress of the Southern Division all the way from Camp Union
to Camp Point Pleasant, and bore tidings of its advance to the
Shawnee capital on the Pickaway Plains, where the assembled
sachems and chiefs had, in their bark council-house in the valley of the
Sciota, resolved upon war against the English Border. Their message
went forth to summon the warriors to arms; this was speedily obeyed
and hundreds of them gathered, ready for the fray. It was the plan
of Cornstalk to defeat the two wings of the army before they could
be united and if Lewis could be beaten and his army destroyed at the
mouth of the Great Kanawha, the men composing the Northern
Division under Dunmore, could be shot down in the narrow defiles of
the valley of the Hockhocking river. All day long that Sunday—October ninth— with silent tread, they approached the Ohio, and late in
the evening, halted in the dense forest in the valley of Campaign creek
near the site of the present village of Addison, in Gallia county, Ohio,
and distant about three miles above the mouth of the Great Kanawha.
Soon after dark the warrors began crossing the Ohio on rafts, seventy-
nine of these having been prepared previously. To ferry so many
over this wide stream on these clumsy transports, must have required
a considerable time. But before morning they were all on the southern bank on the site of "Old Shawane Town" a former home of the
Shawnees, near the mouth of Old Town creek and distant about
three miles from Camp Point Pleasant; and were ready to proceed
to action. Their route lay down through the bottom lands on the east
bank of the Ohio. Here was a heavy growth of timber with a foliage
so dense, as in many places to intercept, in a great measure, the light
of the moon and the stars. Beneath lay many trunks of fallen trees
strewed in different directions and in various stages of decay. The

1. "Documentary History of Dunmore's War," p. 258. Original in the library
of the State Historical Society of Wisconsin.

whole surface of the ground was covered with a luxuriant growth of weeds interspersed with close-set thickets of spice-wood and other undergrowth. A journey through this in the night must have been tedious, tiresome, dark and dreary. The Indians, however, entered upon it promptly and pursued it until break of day. When, about a mile distant from the camp of the sleeping Virginians, one of those unforseen incidents occurred which so often totally defeat or greatly mar the best concerted military plans. This was the discovery by the Virginians of the advancing Indian line, a most fortunate occurrence for, by it, the whole army was saved from destruction; because it was the design of the Indians to have attacked them at break of day, and to force all whom they could not kill, into the two rivers. Had that vast barbarian column swept down in the darkness of the morning upon Lewis' army of sleeping Virginians, it would have been doomed not only to defeat but to total destruction.

THE BEGINNING OF THE BATTLE:—In the gray dawn of the morning twilight, Monday, October 10th, two young men went up along the east bank of the Ohio in quest of deer.[2] When in the narrowest portion of land between Crooked creek and the Ohio river, they were discovered by the Indians, who were advancing in solid phalanx toward the camp of the Virginians. They fired upon the hunters, one of whom they killed, and the other ran into camp and gave the alarm. Instantly the drums beat to arms, and the backwoodsmen rolled out of their blankets, started from the ground, looked to their flints and priming, and were ready on the moment.

---

2. Captain John Stuart says: Two young men were sent out early to hunt for deer, and when up the river (Ohio) two or three miles, they fell on the camp of Indians who fired on them. One was killed; the other escaped and got into camp just before sunrise. He stopped before my tent, and I discovered a number of men collecting around him as I lay in my bed; I jumped up and approached him to know what was the cause of alarm; when I heard him declare that he had seen about five acres of land covered with Indians as thick as they could stand one besides the other."—"Stuart's *Memoirs of the Indian Wars and Other Occurrences.*" p. 46.

"These were Joseph Hughy, of Shelby's company, and James Mooney, of Russell's. The former was killed by a white renegade, Tavenor Ross, while the latter brought the news to camp."—Note by Reuben G. Thwaites, in *Documentary History of Dunmore's War.*" p. 272.

Haywood, the Historian of Tennessee, says that those who discovered the Indians. were James Robertson, and Valentine Sevier, sergeants in Captain Evan Shelby's company. He adds: "It fell to the lot of men from East Tennessee to make an unexpected discovery of the enemy and by that means save from destruction the whole army of Provincials, for it was the design of the enemy to have attacked them at day-dawn and then to have forced all they could not kill, into the two rivers."—"*Civil and Political History of Tennessee.*" p. 58.

ISAAC SHELBY'S ACCOUNT OF THE BATTLE.

The following description of the battle was written on the field, October 16th—six days thereafter—by Isaac Shelby,[3] a Lieutenant in Captain Evan Shelby's company, which he commanded after his father assumed the chief command. It was addressed while on the field to an uncle, John Shelby, on the Watauga river, "for the satisfaction of the people" in that region:—

"On Monday morning, about half an hour before sun-rise, two of Captain Russell's Company discovered a large party of Indians about a mile from Camp, one of which men was shot down by the Indians, the other made his escape and brought the intelligence. In two or three minutes after, two of Captain Shelby's came in and confirmed the account. General Andrew Lewis being informed thereof, immediately ordered out Colonel Charles Lewis to take the command of one hundred and fifty of the Augusta Troops, and with him went Captain Dickinson, Captain Harrison, Captain Wilson, Captain John Lewis, of Augusta, and Captain Lockridge, which made the first Division. Colonel Fleming was also ordered to take the command of one hundred and fifty more of the Botetourt, Bedford, and Fincastle Troops, viz: Captain Thomas Buford, from Bedford, Captain Love, of Botetourt, Captain Shelby and Captain Russell, of Fincastle, which made the second Division. Colonel Charles Lewis's Division marched to the right some distance from the Ohio; and Colonel Fleming, with his Division, on the bank of the Ohio, to the left. Colonel Charles Lewis's Division had not marched quite half a mile from Camp, when, about sun-rise, an attack was made on the front of his Division, in a most vigorous manner, by united tribes of Indians, Shawnees, Delawares, Mingoes, Tawas, (Ottawas) and of several other Nations, in

---

3. Lieutenant Isaac Shelby, son of Captain Evan Shelby, and whose account of the battle, is regarded by historians as the best of all that was written on the field, was born near North Mountain, Maryland, December 11, 1750. He received a common English education, and with his father's family removed to King's Meadows, now Bristol, Tennessee, in 1771. The year after the battle of Point Pleasant, he was engaged in surveying in Kentucky; then became prominent in the Indian wars; then served in the Virginia State Line in the Revolution; in 1792, when Kentucky was admitted into the Union, he was almost unanimously elected first Governor of that State. He was again elected Governor in 1812; commanded Kentucky troops under General Harrison in the second war with England; and in 1817, was tendered the post of Secretary of War, a position which he declined. He died near Stanford, Kentucky, July 18, 1826, fifty-two years after the battle of Point Pleasant, a victory he and his father did so much to win.

number not less than eight hundred, and by many thought to be a thousand. In this heavy attack, Colonel Charles Lewis received a wound, which in a few hours caused his death,[4] and several of his men fell on the spot. In fact, the Augusta Division was forced to give way to the heavy fire of the enemy. In about a second of a minute after the attack on Colonel Lewis's Division, the enemy engaged the front of Colonel Fleming's Division, on the Ohio, and in a short time the Colonel received two balls through his left arm, and one through his breast and after animating the officers and soldiers in a most calm manner, to the pursuit of victory, retired to the Camp.[5] This loss from the field was sensibly felt by the officers in particular; but the Augusta Troops being shortly reinforced from the Camp by Colonel Field, with his Company, together with Captain McDowell, Captain Matthews, and Captain Stuart, from Augusta, Captain John Lewis, Captain Pauling, Captain Arbuckle, and Captain McClennahan, from Botetourt, the enemy, no longer able to maintain their ground, was forced to give way till they were in a line with the troops, which Colonel Fleming had left in action on the bank of the Ohio. In this precipitate retreat,

4. Several statements have been made regarding the death of Colonel Charles Lewis. The following are from eye-witnesses. Captain John Stuart says: "Just as the sun was rising, a heavy fire soon commenced, and Colonel Lewis was mortally wounded, but walked into camp and died a few minutes afterward, observing to Colonel Charles Simms with his last words that he had sent one of the enemy to eternity before him."—Stuart's *Memoirs of the Indian Wars and Other Occurrences.*" p. 46.

"Colonel Lewis was shot in clear ground, as he had not yet taken a tree, while speaking to his men to come on. He turned and handed his gun to a man and walked to camp, telling the men as he passed along, "I am wounded, but go you on and be brave."—*Documentary History of Dunmore's War*," p. 265.

Three members of the Augusta Regiment—Joseph Mayse, Andrew Reed, and James Ellison—all in the column led out by Colonel Lewis,—told Samuel Kercheval the historian of the Shenandoah Valley that: "Colonel Charles Lewis, who had arrayed himself in a gorgeous scarlet waistcoat, (that of the British uniform) against the advice of his friends, thus rendering himself a conspicuous mark for the Indians, was mortally wounded early in the action; yet was able to walk back, after receiving the wound, into his own tent, where he expired. He was met on his way by the Commander-in-Chief, his brother, General Andrew Lewis, who remarked to him: "I expected something fatal would befall you," to which the wounded officer camly replied, "It is the fate of war," and died.—Kercheval's "History of the Valley," pp. 101, 102.

5. "Colonel Fleming was shot with three balls; two in the left arm and one in the left breast, while speaking to his division in a piece of clear ground; with great coolness and deliberation, he stept slowly back and told them not to mind him but to go up and fight."—*Documentary History of Dunmore's War.*" p. 265.

"Fleming was a heroic officer; after two balls had passed through his arm, he continued on the field, and exercised his command with the greatest coolness and presence of mind. His voice was continually heard, "Don't lose an inch of ground; advance; outflank the enemy; keep between them and the river." This was his last command; there came a shot which passed through his lungs and he fell, but insisted still to be permitted to remain upon the field. As he was borne from the field a portion of the lung protruded from the wound, and he pressed it back with his own hand."—Drake's "*History and Biography of the Indians of North America.*" Book V., p. 43.

Colonel Field was killed.[6] During this time, which was till after twelve o'clock, the action continued extremely hot. The close under-wood, many steep banks and logs, greatly favored their retreat; and the bravest of their men made the best use of them whilst others were throwing their dead into the Ohio, and carrying off their wounded. After twelve, the action in a small degree abated, but continued, ex-cept at short intervals, sharp enough till after one o'clock. Their long retreat gave them a most advantageous spot of ground, from whence it appeared to the officers so difficult to dislodge them, that it was thought most advisable to stand, as the line was then formed, which was about a mile and a quarter in length, and had sustained till then a constant and equal weight of the action, from wing to wing. It was till about half an hour of sunset they continued firing on us scattering shots, which we returned to their disadvantage. At length night coming on, they found a safe retreat. They had not the satis-faction of carrying off any of our men's scalps, save one or two strag-glers, whom they killed before the engagement. Many of their dead they scalped, rather than we should have them; but our troops scalped upwards of twenty of their men that were first killed. It is beyond doubt their loss in number, far exceeds ours, which is considerale.[7]

COLONEL WILLIAM FLEMING'S ACCOUNT OF THE BATTLE.

Colonel William Fleming's Orderly Book has the following account of the battle:—

Monday, October the 10th., 1774.

"This morning before sunrise two men came running into Camp and gave information that a considerable body of Indians were in-camped about two miles up the Ohio a small distance from it, who made a very formidable appearance. This important intelligence was very quickly confirmed by two or three more. The drums by order immediately beat to Arms and 150 men were ordered to be paraded

---

6. "Colonel Field was killed behind a great tree, (who) was looking for an Indian who was talking to amuse him, whilst some others were above him on his right hand among some logs, who shot him dead."—"Documentary History of Dunmore's War." p. 265.

7. Shelby's Letter is printed substantially in the "American Archives"; Fourth Series, Vol. I., p. 1016; and completely in the "Documentary History of Dun-more's War." p. 269, etc.

out of each line and march against the enemy in two columns. The right column headed by Colonel Charles Lewis with Captains Dickinson, Harrison and Skidmore. The left column commanded by Colonel Fleming with Captains Shelby, Russell, Love and Buford. Thus disposed they marched pretty briskly about one hundred and fifty or two hundred yards apart up the river about half a mile when on a sudden the enemy lurking behind bushes and trees gave the Augusta line a heavy fire which was briskly followed by a second and third and returned again by our men with much bravery and courage. This attack was attended with the death of some of our bravest officers and men also with the deaths of a great number of the enemy. Nor were the enemy less tardy in their attack upon the left Column; for immediately after the fire upon the right line succeeded a heavy one on the left and a return from us with spirit and resolution. As the disposition in which the men were first placed would never promise success against an Indian enemy, the men were forced to quit their ranks and fly to trees in doing this the enemy made a small advance and forced our men of both lines to retreat the distance of perhaps one or two hundred yards under heavy fires attended with dismal yells and screams from the enemy. About this time we were succored with a detachment from the Camp commanded by Captains Mathews, McDowell, and others of the Augusta line and some time afterwards by all the Captains of each line except Captain McClennahan of Augusta who was upon guard and Captain Lewis of Botetourt, who was ordered to form a line round the Camp for its defence. With the re-enforcement from the camp our men found their strength much increased and making a fierce onset, forced the enemy from their stations and caused them to retreat by degrees about a mile, giving them many brisk fires and hitting many of the leading men as was imagined. We at last with difficulty dislodged them from a fine long ridge leading from a small slash near the river towards the hills and being discontinued by a small wet bottom again rose and was continued to the hills half a mile or more from the river. This advantageous post being gained about one o'clock, all the efforts of the enemy to regain it proved fruitless. Though they would summon all the force they could raise and make many pushes to break the line;

the advantage of the place and the steadiness of the men defied their most furious essays. About three or four o'clock, the enemy growing quite dispirited and all attempts of their warriors to rally them proving vain, they carried off their dead and wounded, giving us now and then a shot to prevent a pursuit; so that about an hour by sun we were in full possession of the field of Battle. Victory having now declared in our favour, we had orders to return in slow pace to our Camp carefully searching for the dead and wounded and to bring them in, as also the scalps of the enemy. The day being by this time far advanced with (out) any written orders, double guards were ordered to be mounted. That night the Parole was "Victory."[8]

CAPTAIN JOHN STUART'S ACCOUNT.

Captain John Stuart,[9] of the Botetourt Regiment, who participated in the battle, says:—

"General Lewis immediately ordered out a detachment of Augusta troops, under his brother, Colonel Charles Lewis, and another detachment of the Betetourt troops, under Colonel William Fleming. These were composed of the companies commanded by the oldest captains; and the junior captains were ordered to stay in camp to aid the others as occasion would require. The detachments marched out in two lines, and met the Indians in the same order of march, about four hundred yards from our camp, and in sight of the guard. The

---

8. Fleming's "Orderly-Book," printed in "Documentary History of Dunmore's War," pp. 313, 360.
9. John Stuart, one of the most remarkable men whose name is connected with frontier history, was born in Augusta county, Virginia, in 1749. He came over the mountains in 1769 to find a home when only nineteen years of age and settled in the "Rich Lands" of what became Greenbrier county, West Virginia. He commanded a company in the Botetourt County Regiment, and was one of the most prominent actors in the battle of Point Pleasant. From thence he accompanied the army to the Pickaway Plains in the Scioto Valley, and was present when the two divisions of the army were united. He witnessed the murder of Cornstalk at Point Pleasant in 1777. He led the relief from Lewisburg, that saved Fort Donnally, ten miles from that place, when besieged by the Indians in 1778. He rose to the rank of Colonel in the Military establishment of Virginia, and was engaged in the Indian wars until their close in 1795. In 1788, he was one of the Delegates from Greenbrier county to the Virginia Federal Convention which ratified the National Constitution, for which he voted. He was a man of culture and refinement and for that day possessed an excellent education. He was a member of "The American Philosophical Society," and of other learned bodies. He was clerk of the county court of Greenbrier county from 1780, to 1807—a period of twenty-seven years. His wife was Agatha, the widow of John Frogge, who was killed in the battle of Point Pleasant. He died August 23, 1823, fifty years after the battle, and because of his writings regarding that and other events, may be designated as the "Historian of Dunmore's War."

Indians made the first fire and killed both the scouts in front of the two lines. Just as the sun was rising, a very heavy fire soon commenced, and Colonel Lewis was mortally wounded. During his life it was his lot to have frequent skirmishes with the Indians, in which he was always successful; had gained much applause for his intrepidity, and was greatly beloved by his troops. Colonel Fleming was also wounded; and our men had given way some distance before they were reinforced by the other companies issuing in succession from the camp. The Indians in turn had to retreat, until they formed a line behind logs and trees, across from the bank of the Ohio to the bank of the Kanawha, and kept up their fire 'till sundown."[10]

General Lewis now knew that if the battle was not ended before darkness settled down upon the field, it would be a night of massacre, or the morrow a day of great doubt, and he resolved to throw a body of men into the rear of the Indian army. He therefore sent three of the most renowned companies on the field to execute this movement. They were those of Captains George Mathews, John Stuart, and Evan Shelby, the latter now commanded by his son, Lieutenant Isaac Shelby, the father having become the chief field officer after the fall of Colonels Lewis, Fleming and Field. They were called from the front to the point where the two rivers meet, and then proceeded under cover of the bank of the Great Kanawha for three quarters of a mile to the mouth of Crooked creek; and thence along the bed of its tortuous course, to their destination; there they ascended the high bluff bank about where Tenth Street, in the town of Point Pleasant now is, and poured a destructive fire upon the Indian rear; and they believing that this was the long expected re-enforcement, under Colonel Christian, gave way, falling back toward the place from which they came that morning.

General Lewis took another precaution against a disastrous defeat. At three o'clock in the afternoon, he sent messengers up the Great Kanawha river to inform Colonel Christian that he was hotly engaged, and to request him to hasten to his assistance. They met that officer about twelve miles from the battlefield, near the site of the present town of Leon, in Cologne Magisterial District, in Mason coun-

---

10. "Memoirs of the Indian Wars and Other Occurrences," p. 46.

ty—His march was quickened, but it was eleven o'clock that night when his troops came upon the field, and the battle had been fought and won. All was quiet save the groans of the wounded, for "only the dead could rest in such a night as that."

On the field the Indians left twenty-three guns; eighty blankets; twenty-seven tomahawks, with match-coats, skins, shot-pouches, powder-horns and war-clubs, which were sold for about £100:00:0.

VIRGINIANS KILLED IN THE BATTLE.

Careful estimates, made from the most authentic documentary evidence extant, place the number killed at eighty-one. The following is a list of names of persons known to have been among the slain, together with the organization to which each belonged:

FIELD OFFICERS.

COLONEL CHARLES LEWIS, commanding the Augusta County Regiment.
COLONEL JOHN FIELD, of the Culpeper County Company.
CAPTAIN JOHN MURRAY, of the Botetourt County Regiment.
CAPTAIN ROBERT MCCLENNAHAN, of the Botetourt County Regiment.
CAPTAIN SAMUEL WILSON, of the Augusta County Regiment.
CAPTAIN CHARLES WARD, of the Augusta County Regiment.

SUBALTERN OFFICERS.

LIEUTENANT HUGH ALLEN, of Captain George Mathews' Company, of the Augusta County Regiment.
LIEUTENANT JONATHAN CUNDIFF, of Captain Thomas Buford's Company, of Bedford County Riflemen.
ENSIGN MATHEW BRACKEN, of Captain Robert McClennahan's Company, of the Botetourt County Regiment.
ENSIGN SAMUEL BAKER, of Captain Henry Pauling's Company, of the Botetourt County Regiment.

PRIVATES.

JOHN FROGG, a sutler, of the Augusta County Regiment.
MARK WILLIAMS, ROGER TOPP and JOSEPH HUGHEY, of Captain Evan Shelby's Company, of the Fincastle County Battalion.
JAMES MOONEY and ———— HICKMAN, of Captain William Russell's Company, of the Fincastle County Battalion.
GEORGE CAMERON, of Captain George Mathews' Company, of the Augusta County Regiment.
SAMUEL CROLEY: Organization to which he belonged not known.

To these add sixty-four others of whom either the name or organization to which they belonged or both are unknown.

The day after the battle, the bodies of the men slain therein, together with those who died of wounds that night, were buried in different places; the following officers—Colonel Charles Lewis, Colonel John Field, Captain John Murray, Captain Robert McClennahan, Captain Samuel Wilson, Lieutenant Hugh Allen, John Frogg and George Cameron—being laid to rest inside of the Magazine directly on the upper point of land, at the confluence of the rivers—now Tuenda-wee Park. All were interred without the pomp of war, but that day the cheeks of many a hardy Virginia-West Virginia mountaineer were bedewed with tears.

VIRGINIANS WOUNDED IN THE BATTLE.

Captain John Stuart, the historian, who was in the battle, says that one hundred and forty men were wounded; and this statement is verified by documentary evidence yet extant. Ensign James Newell, who kept a journal, himself wounded, says, under date of October 21st—eleven days after the battle: "At Point Pleasant was a stockade, built to secure the wounded men who are dieing daily, and it is a most shocking sight to see their wounds." The following are names of persons known to have been among the wounded:

FIELD OFFICERS.

COLONEL WILLIAM FLEMING, commanding the Botetourt County Regiment.
CAPTAIN JOHN DICKINSON, of the Augusta County Regiment.
CAPTAIN JOHN SKIDMORE, of the Augusta County Regiment.
CAPTAIN THOMAS BUFORD, of the Bedford County Riflemen.

SUBALTERNS.

LIEUTENANT DAVID LAIRD, of the Augusta County Regiment.
LIEUTENANT SAMUEL VANCE, of Captain John Lewis' Company, of the Augusta County Regiment.
LIEUTENANT EDWARD GOLDMAN, of Captain Henry Pauling's Company, of the Botetourt County Regiment.
ENSIGN JAMES NEWELL, of Captain William Herbert's Company, of the Fincastle County Battalion.

PRIVATES.

JOHN STUART, REECE PRICE, JOSEPH HUGHEY, and JOHN McCORMACK, of Captain Evan Shelby's Company, of the Fincastle County Battalion.

JOHN BASDELL and WILLIAM PRINCE, of Captain William Russell's Company, of the Fincastle County Battalion.

THOMAS BAKER, of Captain William Campbell's Company, of the Fincastle County Battalion.

JOHN MCMULLEN, DAVID GLASCOM, JOHN FREELAND, and WILLIAM MORRIS, of Captain Mathew Arbuckle's Company, of the Botetourt County Regiment.

THOMAS HUFF and THOMAS CARPENTER, of Captain John Lewis' Company, of the Botetourt County Regiment.

JAMES ALEXANDER and WILLIAM FRANKLIN, of Captain Philip Love's Company, of the Botetourt County Regiment.

STEPHEN ARNOLD, of Captain John Murray's Company, of the Botetourt County Regiment.

CHARLES KENNISON, WILLIAM CLENDENNIN, and THOMAS FERGUSON, of Captain John Stuart's Company, of the Botetourt County Regiment.

HERRY BOWYER, of Captain James Robertson's Company, of the Fincastle County Battalion.

JAMES CURRY and ALEXANDER STUART, of Captain George Moffat's Company, of the Botetourt County Regiment.

BENJAMIN BLACKBURN, JOSEPH MAYSE, THOMAS PRICE and JAMES ROBINSON, the organization to which they belonged being unknown.

To these add one hundred and six others of whom either names or organization to which they belonged or both are unknown.

The number of Indians killed and wounded[11] could never be known for they were continually carrying off their dead and throwing them into the river. A never-failing characteristic of the dying Red-man was a desire that his body might not fall into the hands of his pale-faced antagonist; and his comrades in battle were wont to bear his body from the field when he had fallen. His loss has been stated at two hundred and thirty-three.[12]

The three men who served in the Augusta Regiment—Joseph Mayse, Andrew Reed, and James Ellison—from whom Samuel Kercheval,

---

11. Pu-kee-she-no a Shawnee, whose name signified "I light from flying" was killed in the battle. He was the noblest warrior that perished there. His wife was a Cherokee woman whose name was Mee-thee-ta-she, which signified "a turtle laying her eggs in the sand." These were the parents of Tecumseh and his brothers Ells-wat-a-wa one who foretells; otherwise the Prophet, and Kum-sha-ka, signifying "A tiger that flies in the air." The mother is said to have transplanted the beautiful Cherokee rose from the banks of the Tennessee to those of the Scioto, whence it has spread far and wide. Their home was on the banks of that river, on the site of the present city of Chillicothe, and there the little son, Tecumseh, but six years of age, played while his father was killed at Point Pleasant."— Drake's "Biography and History of the Indians of North America." Book V., p. 123.

12. "American Archives," 4th Series Vol. I., p. 1018.

the historian, obtained his information regarding the battle of Point Pleasant, informed him that some little time after the battle, Indian traders visited the garrison at that place, and stated that "the loss of the Indians in killed and wounded was not short of three hundred warriors."[13]

Captain John Stuart said: "The Indians were exceedingly active in concealing their dead that were killed. I saw a young man draw out three in the heat of the battle * * * The next morning twenty of the enemy were found slain upon the ground. Twelve were afterwards found all concealed in one place; and the Indians confessed that they had thrown a number into the river in time of battle; so that it is possible that the slain on both sides were about equal."[14]

The dead bodies of the Indians who fell in the battle were never buried, but left to decay on the ground where they expired, or to be devoured by the birds and beasts of prey. The Mountain Eagle, lord of the feathered race, while from his lofty flight, with piercing eye, surveyed the varied scenes around and beneath, would not fail to descry the feast prepared for his use. Here he might whet his beak and feast and fatten. Over these, the gaunt wolf, grim tyrant of the forest, might prolong his midnight revelry and howl their funeral dirge; while far remote in the deepest gloom of the wilderness, whither they had fled for safety, the surviving warriors might bewail their fate or chant a requiem to their departed spirits.

There were widely published accounts of the battle of Point Pleasant. The first of these was written by Captain Thomas Slaughter, commanding the Dunmore Volunteers. This he sent to his brother in Culpeper county, who received it November 2d, and the next day, sent it to William Rind and John Pinkney, the publishers of the *Virginia Gazette,* at Williamsburg, in which it was published, November 10, 1774. The *Pennsylvania Gazette* had a full account the following week. The *Royal American Magazine* of Boston, Massachusetts, contained details of the battle in its November No. pp. 438, 439. The first account received in Europe, went across the ocean in the good ship "Harriott," Captain Lee. She touched at Falmouth, England, where the New York mails were landed, and the *London Daily Advertiser,* in January 1775, had a lengthy article on the battle. The

13. "History of the Shenandoah Valley," p. 102.
14. "Memoirs of the Indian Wars and Other Occurrences," p. 46.

same week the Belfast, (Ireland) *News Letter* published it; and that month (January) the *Scots Magazine,* published in Edinburg, Scotland, had a full account thereof. Contempory with this, *The Gentlemen's Magazine* and *Historical Chronicle,* Vol. XLV., January No. pp. 42, 43, of London, contained full details, including lists of killed and wounded. French and German newspapers on the Continent, likewise, published extended articles descriptive of the battle. Thus it was, that, notwithstanding there were then no telegraph lines, no ocean cables, nor steamships, yet because of its importance, details of the great battle, were published practically all over the civilized world.

CHAPTER VI.

The Indians, defeated at Point Pleasant, fled from the field at sundown and crossed the Ohio on the same rafts which brought them over the preceeding night. Thence they trod the long, wearisome journey through the lonely wilderness to their towns on the Pickaway Plains. There Cornstalk called a council of his nation to consult on what was to be done. He upbraided the other chiefs for their folly in not permitting him to make peace before the battle. "What" said he, "Will you do now? The Big Knife (the Virginians) is coming on us, and we shall all be killed. Now you must fight or we are undone." But no one made answer. He then said, "let us kill all our women and children and go and fight till we die." But none would answer. At length he rose and struck his tomahawk in the post in the center of the council house; "I'll go," said he and "make peace;" and the warriors all grunted "ough, ough, ough," and runners were instantly dispatched to the Governor's army to solicit peace and the interposition of the Governor in their behalf.[1]

On the morning of the 12th of October—the second day after the battle—General Lewis, sent James Fowler, James McAnore, and Samuel Huff to Dunmore with a full account of the battle. But this he did not receive, for having sent a messenger to General Lewis with a request to meet him at the Pickaway Plains, he left a garrison of one hundred men at Fort Gower, and with twelve hundred, without a knowledge of the battle, took up the line of march October 11th, up the Hockhocking Valley which he followed by way of the present town of Athens, Ohio, and thence to

---

1. This was related by Cornstalk to a council of officers at Point Pleasant, November 10, 1777, less than an hour before his death—Stuart's *"Memoirs of the Indian War and Other Occurrences."* p. 62.

where the town of Logan, in that State, now stands; from here he
crossed the highland between the valleys of the Hockhocking and the
Scioto rivers, and proceeded towards his destination—the Pickaway
Plains.

Before arriving in the vicinity of the Indian towns, and when fifteen miles distant therefrom, he was met by Mathew Eliott, a white
man, bearing a flag of truce, and accompanied by several Indian
chiefs who requested the assistance of an interpreter through whom
they could communicate with Lord Dunmore. Captain John Gibson,
commanding a company in the "West Augusta Battalion" was designated for this purpose. It was thus learned that Cornstalk and other
chiefs, desired to treat for peace, and requested that Dunmore halt
his army until terms could be agreed upon. Captain Gibson was sent
forward to speak with them,[2] but the army marched onward and on
Monday, October 17th, on a spot, now in the southwest quarter of Section Twelve, of Range twenty-one, in Pickaway Township, Pickaway
county, Ohio, fixed his encampment, to which he gave the name of
"Camp Charlotte," in honor of his wife, the Lady Dunmore, whose
given name was Charlotte.

The next day preliminary arrangements were made. Dunmore was
the presiding officer; Major John Connelly, Secretary; Captain John
Gibson, and Thomas Nicholson, interpreters; and Major Thompson
was chief officer of the day. On the 19th, Lord Dunmore admitted
the chieftains to a conference. It was a great day away out in that
western wilderness. White and Red men met to consummate a treaty
of peace, after a march of two thousand four hundred men from the
heart of Virginia to the center of the then known American wilderness. As the head official of that army and as the presiding officer of
that convention, there sat a royal Colonial Governor, a Lord, a Peer
of Great Britain, who had sat for ten years in the House of Lords,
and had now walked on foot,[2] from the Shenandoah Valley to the
banks of the Scioto. There too, was Colonel Adam Stephen, Colonel
William Crawford, Major Angus McDonald, Captain George Rogers
Clark, Captain John Gibson, Captain Daniel Morgan, Captain James

2. See affidavit of Captain John Gibson, in Jefferson's "Notes on Virginia."
Appendix, p. 16.
2. "American Archives." Fourth Series, Vol II., pp. 310, 312.

Parsons, and many others who were to be future history makers. And there was Cornstalk, the foremost warrior of his race, who, in tones that rang out over the Pickaway Plains, electrified his hearers, and told of the wrongs which his people had suffered, detailed their woes, and afterward quietly submitted to the terms offered, and entered into a treaty which, three years later, at Point Pleasant, he sacrificed his life to maintain. The next day Lord Dunmore submitted to the Convention what he called "THE TERMS OF OUR RECONCILIATION." These afterward known as the terms of the treaty of Camp Charlotte[3] and to which the Indians agreed, were as follows:

I. To give up, without reserve all the prisoners ever taken by them in war with the white people; and to never again wage war against the frontier of Virginia.

II. To give up all negroes taken by them from white people since the last war; and to pay for all property destroyed by them in that time.

III. To surrender all horses and other valuable effects which they had taken from the white people since the last war.

IV. To no more in the future hunt on or visit the south side of the Ohio river, except for the purpose of trading with the white people.

V. To no more molest boats of white people, while descending or ascending the Ohio river.

VI. To agree to such regulations for trade with the white people as should hereafter be dictated by the King's instruction.

VII. To deliver up hostages as a guarantee for the faithful compliance with the terms of the treaty; to be kept by the Whites until convinced of the sincerity on the part of the Indians to adhere to all these articles.

VIII. To have from the Governor a guarantee that no white people should be permitted to hunt on the northern, or Indian side of the Ohio river.

IX. To meet at Pittsburg the next spring and enter into a supplemental treaty by which the terms of the treaty of "Camp Charlotte" should be ratified and fully confirmed.

In consideration of an agreement with these covenants, Lord Dunmore gave them every promise of protection and good treatment on the part of the Virginians.

---

3. For data relating to the terms of the treaty of "Camp Charlotte" see Bancroft's "History of the United States." Vol. IV., p. 88; "Documentary History of Dunmore's War." pp. 304, 386; "Journal of the Continental Congress," Vol. II., pp. 174, 175, 183, 251. Journal of the "House of Burgesses" of Virginia, Session beginning June 1, 1775; Thwaites and Kellogg's "Revolution on the Upper Ohio." pp. 25-127; and Windsor's "Narrative and Critical History of America." Vol. VI., p. 114.

ADVANCE OF GENERAL LEWIS' ARMY TO THE PICKAWAY PLAINS:—
On the 11th of October, General Lewis received orders issued on the
day of battle by the Earl of Dunmore to cross the Ohio with his
army, and proceed to the Pickaway Plains, there to meet the right
wing marching from Fort Gower. But Lewis could not obey this
command. The dead were to be buried, and this was done on the 11th
of October; Colonel Christian must send a company to bring in the
cattle which he had left on the Great Kanawha, and this he did on the
12th; the store-house and breast-works must be provided for the supplies and the protection of the wounded, and this work was progressing
on the 13th. Because of the loss of officers in the battle, there must be
re-organization in the army, and this took place on the 14th, when
Lieutenant William McKee succeeded to the command of Captain
John Murray's company; Lieutenant Givens to that of Captain Samuel Wilson; and Lieutenant William McCoy to that of Captain Robert
McClennahan. Additional supplies must be received, and these arrived on the evening of the 14th, being brought from the mouth of
Elk river by Captain Thomas Slaughter, with his Dunmore Volunteers. The horses which were stampeded on the day of the battle, had
to be collected, and on the 15th, three men were detailed from each
company, and under the command of three Sergeants were sent out for
this purpose—one to go four miles up the Ohio; another up the
Great Kanawha to the "first narrows" (mouth of Three-mile creek)
and the third "to take the ridges" between the two rivers. On the
16th, the horses were gathered in, and sixty selected to carry flour;
then two were assigned to each company to carry "tents and bundles."
Colonel Fleming, though desperately wounded, was appointed commander of the post. Officers left were Captains Dickinson, (wounded)
Lockridge, Herbert and Slaughter; and Lieutenants Draper and Vance
and Ensign Smith. The garrison was composed of men detailed from
the various organizations, who were formed into companies; by Captains Lockridge, Herbert and Slaughter. It consisted of four lieutenants, four ensigns, fifteen sergeants, one drummer one fifer, and
two hundred and fifty privates, making a total of two hundred and
seventy-eight men. At length all was in readiness, and on the evening
of the 17th of October, General Lewis crossed the Ohio with one

thousand, one hundred and fifty men, with ten days rations, Sixty-one pack-horses, and one hundred and eighteen beeves, and encamped on the site of the present town of Kanauga, in Gallia county, Ohio. The next morning fifteen additional beeves were taken over; and then the march along the Ohio, and thence up the valley of Champaign creek, still in Gallia county, was continued for six miles when an encampment was made for the night.   Onward marched the army until the 22nd., when it arrived on the banks of Kinnickinnick creek, now in the northeastern portion of Ross county, Ohio, distant fifteen miles from Camp Charlotte.   Here he, (Lewis,) received the first information of the treaty.   It was conveyed to him by the hands of White-fish, an Indian chief, in the form of a communication from Lord Dunmore.   From here Lewis's army proceeded to Congo creek, distant four and one half miles from Camp Charlotte, where it arrived on the 23rd, and went into camp on what is now the southeast quarter of Section Thirty, in Pickaway Township, Pickaway county, Ohio,[4]

The following statements, the first by General Lewis, the second by Captain John Stuart, the historian, both of whom were present, explain in a most interesting manner, the meeting of General Lewis and his Lordship, on this occasion:

"October 29th, Saturday:—General Lewis returned to Camp Point Pleasant from the Northwest of the Ohio, and explained to the wounded Colonel Fleming how he met Lord Dunmore at the Pickaway Plains.   'He stated that when near the Indian towns, an express came from Lord Dunmore with the information that he had very nearly concluded a peace, and for General Lewis to halt his troops. The place being inconvenient to encamp, he marched on in quest of a more suitable spot. Another messenger arrived saying that the Shawnees had agreed to the terms of Lord Dunmore; that peace was in a manner concluded; and an invitation was extended to General Lewis and other officers of the southern wing to visit his camp. Lewis proposed to march the southern wing to his Lordship's camp, but the guide mistook the path and followed one leading between the Indian towns and the Governor's camp. This put the Indians into a fright, they believing that General Lewis would attack their towns, and they left his Lordship and ran off. Lord Dunmore, then, accompanied by Colonel John Gibson, and White-fish, an Indian, rode over to Lewis' camp. Dunmore then asked Lewis if he proposed

---

4. "History of Franklin and Pickaway counties" (Ohio) p. 265.

to march to the Indian towns. Colonel Lewis assured him that he had no thought of attacking the towns after receiving his Lordship's orders."[5]

Captain John Stuart the historian, who was present, thus tells of the visit of Lord Dunmore to General Lewis's camp:

"When the Governor reached General Lewis's camp, his Lordship requested that officer to introduce him to his officers; and we were accordingly ranged in rank and had the honor of an introduction to the Governor and Commander-in-Chief, who politely thanked us for services rendered on so momentous occasion, and assured us of his high esteem and respect for our conduct."[6]

Captain Stuart speaking of this meeting, says further:

"On the Governor's consulting General Lewis, it was deemed necessary that a garrison should be established at the mouth of the Great Kanawha to intercept and prevent the Indians from crossing the Ohio to our side; also to prevent any whites from crossing over to the side of the Indians; and by such means to preserve a future peace according to the conditions of the treaty thus being made by the Governor with the Indians."[7]

Governor Dunmore having informed General Lewis that the Shawnees had agreed to all his terms and that the presence of the left wing of the army could be of no service, "but rather a hindrance to the peace being concluded," now ordered him to return, and on the next day, his army began to retrace its steps back to the Ohio. Thus ended the connection of the Southern Division with the treaty of Camp Charlotte.

THE TREATY IN PROGRESS:—Dunmore now urged promptness on the part of the chieftains, saying that if the war was to be ended by a treaty, he was anxious to proceed with it at once, otherwise, he would be forced to resume hostilities. Logan, the Mingo chief returned at this juncture from an incursion into the settlements in the valleys of the Holston and Clinch rivers. Lord Dunmore dispatched two intrepeters to invite him to attend the treaty. To this he replied by saying:—"I am a warrior, not a councillor, and shall not come." His people, the Mingoes, whose towns were on site of the present city of Columbus, the capital of Ohio, were much displeased with the terms of peace dictated by Dunmore and resolved to slip away from the treaty. When his Lordship learned this he determined

5. Fleming's Orderly Book in "Documentary History of Dunmore's War." p. 356.
6. "Memoirs of the Indian Wars and Other Occurrences," p. 57.
7. "Memoirs of the Indian Wars and Other Occurrences," p. 57, 58.

to prevent it and placed the matter in the hands of Colonel William
Crawford, who writing Colonel George Washington under date of
November 14, 1774, says:—

"Lord Dunmore ordered myself with two hundred and forty men to
set out in the night. We were to march to a town about forty miles
distant from our camp, up the Scioto, where we understood the whole
of the Mingoes were to rendezvous upon the following day, in order to
pursue their journey. This intelligence came by John Montour, son of
Captain Montour, whom you formerly knew.

Because of the number of Indians in our camp we marched out of it
under pretense of going to Hockhocking for more provisions. Few knew
of our setting off anyhow, and none knew where we were going to until
next day. · Our march was performed with as much speed as possible.
We arrived at a town called the Salt-Lick Town the ensuing night,
and at daybreak we got around it with one-half our force, and the remainder were sent to a small village half a mile distant. Unfortunately
one of our men was discovered by an Indian who lay out from town
some distance by a log which the man was creeping up to. This obliged
the man to kill the Indian. This happened before daylight which did us
much damage, as the chief part of the Indians made their escape in the
dark; but we got fourteen prisoners, and killed six of the enemy, wound-
ing several more. We got all their baggage and horses, ten of their guns,
and 200 (two) hundred white prisoners. The plunder sold for four hundred pounds sterling, besides what was returned to a Mohawk that was
there. The whole of the Mingoes were ready to start, and were to have set
out the morning we attacked them."[8]

This was the only fighting done by the right wing of the army during the war. At length the treaty closed with the understanding that,
for "the sake of greater solemnity," a supplemental one should be held
at Pittsburg the next spring. The Shawnees delivered as hostages, as
a guarantee for good behavior, and a compliance with the terms of the
treaty, five of their chiefs, of whom Chenusaw, "The Judge." Cutenwa,
and Newau, were three, and they were taken to Williamsburg, the capital of Virginia. Dunmore likewise conveyed twelve warriors of the
Mingoes, to be detained at Pittsburg.

THE RETURN OF THE ARMY:—The southern Division under General
Lewis left the Pickaway Plains on the 25th of October; two days
later, several men returned to Point Pleasant and brought the first

---

8. The "Washington-Crawford Letters." p. 55.

intelligence of the treaty.   On the 28th, numbers of the troops arrived at the same place; and the next day General Lewis with the rear guard came in.   Here the left wing practically disbanded.   Colonel Christian writing Colonel Preston under date of November 8th, says:

"I dare say the Army is now scattered from Elk—now Charleston, West Virginia—to Camp Union;" perhaps from Point Pleasant to the Warm Springs, all in little companies.   Many of the Fincastle men crossed the Ohio at Point Pleasant and intended to steer for Clinch river.   Others by Kellys—that is to the mouth of Kelly's Creek, on the Great Kananwha, twenty miles above the mouth of Elk."[9]

Dunmore's division left Camp Charlotte about the last day of October, and was back at Fort Gower, on the 5th day of November. He detailed a garrison of twenty-five men for Fort ̇Fincastle, at Wheeling, and one hundred to remain at Fort Dunmore; then he hastened homeward by way of the latter place and arrived at Williamsburg on the 4th of December.   From Fort Gower many of the men ʼreturned to their homes by way of the Little Kanawha Valley, and the site of the present town of Clarksburg, West Virginia.   At the Conference of Dunmore and Lewis at the Pickaway Plains, when it was decided to erect a fort at the mouth of the Great Kanawha, it was agreed that Captain William Russell's Company of the Fincastle Battalion should be detailed for this work.   Accordingly, Russell accompanied Dunmore's Northern Division back to Fort Gower, whence he descended the Ohio to Point Pleasant, where he found that nothing had been done on the Fort since General Lewis crossed the Ohio; and the supply of flour was sufficient for only eight days. General Lewis had left a letter for him saying that his Commissary's report showed that he had left one hundred and sixty beeves in the woods at that place, and Russell hoped that his company might get eighty or a hundred of them.[10]   Here Russell constructed a small palisaded rectangular fort about eighty yards long with block-houses at two of its corners, and bestowed upon it the name of "Fort Blair."[11]

Captain Russell was still at Fort Blair in June 1775.   Writing Colonel Fleming at that time, he said:—

"I am this morning preparing to start off the cattle up Big Sandy, and

---

9. "Documentary History of Dunmore's War," p. 306.
10. "Documentary History of Dunmore's War," p. 308.
11. "Documentary History of Dunmore's War," p. 308.

expect (the) command will leave here this Wednesday or Thursday at (the) furtherest; and I shall Decamp myself with a convoy with the other stores next Monday; and expect to overtake the stock at Big Painted Lick about sixty miles up Big Sandy."[12]

At the same time that year, Dunmore discharged the garrisons at Fort Fincastle and Fort Dunmore; and the last men in service in Dunmore's war, returned to their homes.

THE SUPPLEMENTAL TREATY AT PITTSBURG, 1775:—By reference to the ninth article in the terms of the treaty of Camp Charlotte, it was agreed on the part of both parties thereto, that a supplemental convention, or treaty, should be held at Pittsburg, the ensuing spring for the purpose of ratifying and confirming the treaty of Camp Charlotte, and for the further decision of some minute details connected therewith, but which could not receive attention at the hurried meeting on the Pickaway Plains. Lord Dunmore promised that he would, by messenger, inform the chiefs of the several nations when it would be most convenient for him to meet them at Pittsburg, there to complete the work left unfinished at Camp Charlotte.

The House of Burgesses assembled at Williamsburg, June 1, 1775. Five days thereafter, Governor Dunmore sent to it a written message, saying that he was transmitting therewith a paper containing the "Substance of the peace agreed to between me and the Indians which has not been formally ratified; that having been deferred to a meeting intended to be held at Fort Dunmore this spring, when all the Ohio Indians, for the greater solemnity, were to be present, but which I have not been able to find time to proceed to."[13]

The title of this Document was:—

"SUBSTANCE OF THE PEACE AGREED TO BETWEEN THE EARL OF DUNMORE, GOVERNOR OF VIRGINIA, ON THE PART OF THAT COLONY; AND THE CORNSTALK ON THE PART OF THE SHAWNEE INDIANS.

Intended to be ratified at a general meeting of the Ohio Indians, at Fort Dunmore."[14]

This was laid on the table the same day, "to be perused by the

---

12. "Revolution on the Upper Ohio." pp. 13, 14.
13. See Journal of the House of Burgesses, Session beginning Thursday, June 1, 1775.
14. Journal of the House of Burgesses, Session beginning Thursday, June 1, 1775.

members of the House." There it remained until Friday, June 20th, when it was taken up, considered, and a bill passed, entitled "*An Act for appointing Commissioners to ratify and confirm the late treaty of peace with the Ohio Indians.*" With this, the Council of State—a Senate under the Colonial form of government—refused to concur. A Committee of Conference considered the subject; and reported that an address should be presented to the Governor requesting that his "Excellency would appoint persons to ratify the treaty with the Indians; and recommended to the House to vote a sum of money not exceeding two thousand pounds, for that business."[15]

But the next day, June 24th—the last of the session—the members of the house had intelligence from the west to the effect that there was dissatisfaction on the part of the Indians, because of the failure to make provision for the treaty supplementing that of Camp Charlotte. There was hesitation no longer. That body at once took action as follows:—

(*Whereas*) "Certain *Information* having been received of the great discontent of the *Ohio Indians*, by reason of the delay of the Ratification of the late treaty of peace concluded upon by his Excellency the Governor, on the part of this Colony and the *Cornstalk* (at Camp Charlotte) on the part of the said *Indians*, and that the inhabitants on our frontier are under just apprehension of a renewal of an *Indian* war, and no steps having been pursued by his Lordship for carrying on the said treaty, or delivering up the *Indian* Hostages, agreeable to the terms of said treaty:—

(*Therefore*) *Resolved*, That the said treaty be immediately entered upon; and that *George Washington, Thomas Walker, James Wood, Andrew Lewis, John Walker,* and *Adam Stephen*, Esquires, or any three or more of them, be, and they are hereby constituted and appointed, Commissioners, on the part and behalf of this colony, to meet the chiefs or head men of the said Ohio Indians, as soon as the same can be done, at such place as they shall find most proper, to ratify and confirm the said treaty, on the part of this colony, and to demand and receive of the said *Indians* the ratification and full performance of the said treaty on their parts; and that Robert Carter Nicholas, Esquire, Treasurer, or the Treasurer for the time being, shall, and (he) is hereby directed and required to pay all such expenses and charges, out of the public money in his hands, as may be incurred on account of such treaty, provided the

---

15. See Journal of the House of Burgesses, session beginning Thursday, June 1, 1775.

same do not exceed the sum of two thousand pounds, for which the said Commissioners shall account to the next General Assembly."

Ordered, that Mr. Mercer do carry this Resolution to the Council and desire their concurrence.

A message from the Council by Mr. Blair:—

Mr. Speaker.

"The Council have agreed to the Resolve for appointing Commissioners to ratify the treaty of peace with the *Ohio Indians;* and for defraying the expense thereof."[16]

The Commissioners named above, held a meeting the same evening and appointed Captain James Wood, one of their number, to proceed to the Ohio and invite the Indians to a treaty at Pittsburg, on the 12th of September, ensuing. He left Williamsburg, the day after his appointment; spent three days at his home at Winchester in the Shenandoah Valley, and arrived at Pittsburg on the 9th of July. There he met many chiefs of various nations, to all of whom he explained the object of his visit. July 19th, he left Pittsburg and visited the Delawares, Mingoes, Wyandots, Shawnees, and other nations, all of whom he requested to send their chiefs to attend the treaty. He returned to Pittsburg August 11th, having been in the Ohio Wilderness for thirty-four days. His mission was eminently successful. The next day he departed for Winchester, where he arrived on the 17th, ensuing, and from there transmitted his report to the Commissioners, in whose service he had been employed. Now all awaited the coming of the Convention.

Meantime, the people of the "District of West Augusta," appointed a Committee of Safety. It prepared and forwarded a petition to the Continental Congress, and that body on July 12th, decided that there was "too much reason to apprehend that the British Government would spare no pains to excite the several nations of Indians to take up arms against these Colonies;" and that "it becomes us to be very active and vigilant in exerting every prudent means to strengthen and confirm their friendly disposition toward these Colonies." That day three Indian Departments were therefore created—The Southern, Central, and Northern—and it was provided that five Commissioners

---

16. See Journal of the House of Burgesses, Saturday, June 24th, session beginning Thursday, June 1, 1775.

be appointed for the first, and three each for the second and third. On the next day, Benjamin Franklin, James Wilson, and Patrick Henry were unanimously appointed Commissioners for the Central Department, which included all of the Indian nations which had been parties to the treaty of Camp Charlotte. September 14th, ensuing, Lewis Morris, then at Pittsburg, was appointed in place of Benjamin Franklin, who was unable to attend the convention at that place; and the next day, Dr. Thomas Walker, who was one of the Virginia Commissioners, was appointed by the Continental Congress in place of Patrick Henry, who declined to serve. The appointment of these Commissioners by Congress carried therewith, an appropriation of $6,666.63, from the Continental Treasury, for their expenses and the purchase of presents for the Indians.[17]

Because of the tardiness of the Indian chiefs to arrive at Pittsburg, the treaty convention did not convene on September 12th, but, on that date Commissioners of the Continental Congress, as well as those of Virginia, were present. They organized by electing Dr. Thomas Walker, chairman of the Joint Commission, he being a member of both. On the 15th many Indians had arrived and the treaty convention was duly opened, and continued in session until October 19th— a period of thirty-four days—in all of which Thomas Nicholson and his associate interpreters were busy almost day and night. Many chieftains were present—The White Mingo for the Mingoes; Cornstalk, Nimwha, Wryneck, Silver Heels, Blue Jacket, and fifteen other chiefs for the Shawnees; White Eyes, Custaloga, and Captain Pipe, for the Delawares; the Half King for the Wyandots; Flying Crow and Kyashuta for the Six Nations; Shaganaba for the Ottowas; and many other orators of the wilderness. It was by far the largest deliberative congress of Indians that ever assembled in the valley of the Ohio. Every article in the preliminary treaty at Camp Charlotte the preceding autumn, was fully discussed by both Whites and Indians. At length all were agreed to, confirmed and ratified, and when this convention adjourned, every Indian nation from the Upper Allegheny to the Falls of the Ohio,

---

17. See Journal of the Continental Congress. (Ford's Edition) Vol. II., pp. 174, 175, 183, 251.

and from that river to Lake Erie—in short every one of the Confederated Nations of 1771—of those participating in the preliminary treaty of Camp Charlotte, and in the supplemental treaty at Pittsburg—entered into a pledge of peace and friendship, not only to Virginia, but to the New American Nation as well.

CHAPTER VII.

In America at the time the battle of Point Pleasant was fought
and won, a few hundred soldiers decided questions of equal magni-
tude to those which, in Europe, would have called into action on the
field, as many thousands. Thus in this country, issues of vital importance were changed by the results of battles in which apparently
insignificient numbers were engaged. At the same time many thousands of men on battlefields in the old world were necessary to settle questions of far less import. This was due to the difference of
the state of society and of population here and there. The numbers on the field at Point Pleasant, to those acquainted with European
wars, and those of our own country in more recent times, must appear to be very inconsiderable; but such then were conditions as
to society and population, that in the wilds of America, a few
hundred Virginians could, and did decide issues of such mighty
importance and far reaching effects, that historians in a century have
not seen them in their full force and operation. Roosevelt has said:

"Certainly, in all the contests waged against the northwestern Indians
during the last half of the eighteenth century there was no other where
the whites inflicted so great a relative loss on their foes. Its results
were most important. It kept the northwestern tribes quiet for the
first three years of the Revolutionary struggle; and above all it rendered possible the settlement of Kentucky, and therefore the winning of
the west. Had it not been for Lord Dunmore's war, it is more than
likely that when the colonies achieved their freedom, they would have
found their western boundary fixed at the Allegheny Mountains."[1]

The victory won at the battle of Point Pleasant, made possible the
preliminary treaty with the confederated Indian nations at Camp
Charlotte, away out in the Ohio Wilderness. Speaking of it Bancroft
says:—

1. "Winning of the West." Vol. I., p. 240.

"The results inured exclusively to the benefit of America. The Indians desired peace; the rancor of the white people changed to confidence. The royal Governor of Virginia and the Virginian army in the valley of the Scioto nullified the act of parliament which extended the province of Quebec² to the Ohio, and in the name of the King of Great Britain triumphantly maintained for Virginia the western and northwestern jurisdiction which she claimed as her chartered right."³

This treaty led to the supplemental one at Pittsburg, to which there were three parties— the allied Indian Nations, the Government of Virginia, and the Continental Congress. The results were most gratifying. All parties were greatly pleased. A substantial peace had been secured to the Western Border, which was not broken until the spring of 1778—quite three years after the treaty stipulations had been concluded. What did this mean in America? Simply this: There were no Indian wars in these years. The Border men were free from New York to Georgia, and General Gates was thus enabled to collect the American soldiery from the Penobscot to the Savannah, and with this, overthrow Burgoyne at Saratoga. This meant France to the aid of the Colonies; and that meant the Independance of the United States. Does any one believe that if, in 1777, a vast barbarian army, an ally of England, had been carrying desolation and death along the whole frontier of civilization, that Gates could have mustered the men who achieved victory at Saratoga?

Again, at the time of the battle of Point Pleasant, no white man had found a permanent home within the present limits of the State of Kentucky. But the long continued peace with the Indians through treaty stipulations which were made possible by that battle, opened the way for a large imigration to that State within the next three years. Will any one say that if the Shawnees and their confederated nations had been carrying on a relentless warfare against the Virginians, that Kentucky could have been settled at that time? But what of these Kentucky settlements? Did they not form the basis of operations of General George Rogers Clark in his conquest of the

---

2. The "Quebec Act" was passed by the parliament of England June 22, 1774. By its provisions the bounds of the Province of Quebec were so enlarged as to comprise all the country northwest of the Ohio to the heads of Lake Superior and the Mississippi. Thus it was that Quebec was made to include all the present States of Ohio, Indiana, Illinois, Michigan, Wisconsin and a large part of Minnesota; and the treaty of Camp Charlotte was thus negotiated on the soil of Canada.
3. "History of the United States," Vol. IV., p. 88.

Illinois County in 1777-8? And did not this conquest induce the General Assembly of Virginia, in the last mentioned year, to pass an Act creating Illinois County, an Act by which civil government was extended to the Mississippi river? In the treaty Convention of Paris in 1783, whereby the independence of the United States was being recognized, and the western boundary of the new Nation determined, the British representatives voted to place this at the crest of the Alleghenies, and the Spanish representative in that body voted with them. But the Americans stoutly asserted that, not only had they conquered the vast Illinois region, but that Virginia had established civil government therein. So the Mississippi river, and not the Alleghenies, became the western boundary of the United States. Verily, the men who fought the battle of Point Pleasant, were Empire Builders, and the victory achieved by them on that field changed the course of American history.

CHAPTER VIII.

No work with which the author is acquainted contains any reference to the compensation of the soldiers serving in Dunmore's War, or to a settlement of any of the expenses pertaining to it. When on May 14, 1774, the House of Burgesses authorized Governor Dunmore to prosecute the war against the western Indians, it made no provision whatever for meeting the expenses thereof.

In the circular letter of Colonel William Preston, addressed to the people of Fincastle county, July 20, 1774, he urged enlistments for the war; and as an inducement, he said: "The House of Burgesses will, without doubt, enable his Lordship to reward every volunteer in a handsome manner."[1]

Lord Dunmore writing General Lewis from Winchester, July 24th, used the following language:—

"The expense of the numerous scouting parties in the different counties forming an extensive frontier, will soon exceed the expenses of an expedition against the towns which will be more effectual, and we may as well depend on the House of Burgesses providing for the expedition as for a greater expense of action on the defensive. At any rate we know the old law is still in force, (and) as far as it goes, we are sure of being reimbursed."[2]

It was with this assurance of compensation for service that the men of the border enlisted and filled the ranks of both divisions of the army in Dunmore's war. The first session of the House of Burgesses held after its close convened at Williamsburg, Thursday, June 1, 1775. In his written message to this body, that day, Governor Dunmore said:—

"I must recommend to you to fall upon some means for paying the officers and private men employed in repelling the late invasion and in-

1. "Documentary History of Dunmore's War." p. 92.
2. "Documentary History of Dunmore's War." p. 98.

cursions of the Indians, as I make no doubt you will think their services
on that occasion deserving of your attention."[3]

On the third day of the session, the House by resolution, requested
his Lordship to communicate to it:

"The best information he has had respecting the number of the militia
lately drawn into actual service in the defense of this Colony, by his
Excellency's command, and the probable expense attending the same; and
that his Lordship will inform the House, what militia his Excellency has
ordered on duty since the conclusion of the late Indian Expedition and for
what purposes."[4]

June 5th, the Governor made extended reply to this request. In
it he said:—

"I can only from recollection (not having been furnished with exact
returns.) acquaint you that the body of militia which Colonel Andrew
Lewis conducted, and that which I marched in person amounted, together
to about three thousand men, officers included. But I refer you to the
Lieutenants of the counties from whence the militia were drawn   for
that service; to the commanding officers of the different Corps, and to the
Captains under them for the returns and lists of whose respective companies you will obtain the information in regard to number, and from
that of expense which you require, in the best and most particular manner."

With respect to what militia have been ordered on duty since the conclusion of the Indian Expedition, it was thought requisite to continue a
body of one hundred men at a temporary Fort (Fort Blair) near the
mouth of the Great Kanhaway, as well for taking care of the men
who had been wounded in the action between Colonel Andrew Lewis'
Division and the Indians, as for securing that part of the back country
from the attempts of stragling parties of Indians, who might not be ap-
prised of the peace concluded, or others of the tribes which had joined
in it."

"It was likewise necessary to keep up a small body of men at Fort
Dunmore (Pittsburg) in like manner for the security of the Country
on that side, and also for guarding twelve Indian Prisoners belonging
to the Mingo Tribe which had not surrendered or acceded to the peace
concluded, only, with the Shawnese; and seventy-five men were employed
at this place for these purposes."

"Twenty-five men were likewise left at Fort Fincastle (Wheeling) as
a post of communication between the two others, and altogether for the
further purpose of forming a chain on the back of the settlers to observe

3. "Journal of the House of Burgesses." Session beginning June 1, 1775.
4. "Journal of the House of Burgesses." Session beginning June 1, 1775.

the Indians until we shall have good reason to believe nothing more was apprehended from them; which as soon as I received favorable accounts of, I ordered the several Posts to be evacuated and the men to be discharged."[5]

The members of the House of Burgesses were greatly pleased with the interest manifested in his communications concerning the Indian Expedition—Dunmore's War—and that body the same day sent to him an address in which they said:—

"We assure your Lordship that we will pursue the most speedy Measures for defraying the Expenses of the Military Expedition against the Indians. That proper Provision has not yet been made for those gallant officers and Soldiers, who so nobly exposed their Lives in defense of this country cannot be justly imputed to any delay or Neglect on our part, this being the first Opportunity your Lordship hath been pleased to afford us in paying a proper Attention to their signal Services and giving them their due Reward."[6]

Acting in harmony with this declaration, the House on Wednesday, June 19th, passed a Bill entitled "An Act for appointing Commissioners to settle the Accounts of the Militia lately drawn out into actual Service and for making Provision to pay the Same." This was agreed to by the Council of State, two days later, and as a source of revenue, a provision was inserted *imposing a duty on imported slaves.* This Dunmore declared to be in violation of an Act passed in the tenth year of his Lordship's reign, and he vetoed it, saying that he very much "regretted the miscarriage of the Bill I had so much at heart." He offered to send it to the King and request his favorable consideration thereof; but for reasons now to be explained this was not done.

The Revolution was at hand. On the 20th of April preceding, Dunmore removed the powder from the magazine at Williamsburg to a British vessel. Great excitement prevailed; the people took up arms under the leadership of Patrick Henry, and the Governor compromised the matter by paying for the powder. On the 6th of June, he, with his family, went on board the British man-of-war "Fowey" lying in James river. From there he kept in communication with the House of Burgesses. On the 24th of June, his civil

---

5. "Journal of the House of Burgesses," Session beginning June 1, 1775.
6. "Journal of the House of Burgesses," Session beginning June 1, 1775.

administration in Virginia terminated, and the same day, that body adjourned, never to meet, as such, again. Before separating the members resolved to meet in convention, on the 17th day of July, ensuing, in Richmond. This they did, and the convention having organized, proceeded to appoint a general Committee of Safety, consisting of eleven members, which was henceforth the governing body in Virginia, until it became an independent State. The convention also adopted a number of Ordinances which had the force of law. One of these was practically the Act which the House had passed the preceeding month, and which Dunmore had vetoed, the title being "An Ordinance for appointing Commissioners to settle the Accounts of the Militia lately drawn out into actual Service, and for making Provision to Pay the same."

In this Ordinance the action formerly taken by the Governor and House of Burgesses relative to the matter was revived; and it was decided that because the former had thought fit to refuse his assent to the Act passed by the latter, "many of the inhabitants particularly on the frontiers of this colony, are left in the greatest distress, from which there is no prospect of their being relieved but by the intervention of this Convention." It was therefore ordained:

"That Archibald Cary, William Cabell, Colonel William Fleming, John Winn, and John Nicholas be, and they are hereby appointed Commissioners for the counties of Fincastle, Botetourt, Culpeper, Pittsylvania, Halifax and Bedford, and that part of Augusta which lies to the eastward of the Allegheny Mountains; and Richard Lee, Francis Peyton, Josias Clapham, Henry Lee, and Thomas Blackburn, for the other counties, and for that part of the county of Augusta which lies to the westward of the Allegheny Mountains, and for the provinces of Maryland and Pennsylvania,' to examine, state and settle the accounts of such, pay for provisions, arms, and ammunition, and other necessaries furnished the Militia of the counties for which they were appointed Commissioners, and all demands against the colony on account thereof, who shall be allowed £1:05:0 per day each. And the said Commissioners, or any three or more of them shall, and they are hereby empowered and required to meet for the purposes aforesaid at such times and places as they shall respectively think fit and convenient of which public notice shall be advertised at the Court-House of each respective county, at least one

_____

7. It would appear from this that there were volunteers from both the Colonies of Maryland and Pennsylvania, in service in the Northern Division of the army, under Dunmore.—V. A. L.

month before such meeting, and adjourn from time to time until they shall have settled all accounts relating to said Militia."[8]

These Commissioners were required to certify all accounts so examined, stated and settled, to the General Committee of Safety; then six or more members thereof were required to issue warrants on the Treasurer, who was required, on or before the first day of January, 1776, to pay such certified accounts.

For the raising of the money necessary to meet the payments of these bills the rates of taxation were increased, but because of the remote payment of these, Robert Carter Nicholas, Treasurer for the time being, was empowered to issue Treasury Notes for such sum as might be requisite to meet the purposes of the Ordinance, these to be signed by Henry King and John Pendleton.

The rate of compensation per day for the Officers and Privates engaged in the war was fixed as follows:

For the Commanding Officer	£1: 5s. 0d.
For the County Lieutenant	1: 00. 0.
For a Colonel	15: 0.
For a Lieutenant-Colonel	13: 0.
For a Major	12: 0.
For a Captain	10: 0.
For a Lieutenant	7: 6.
For an Ensign	7: 0.
For a Quarter-Master	6: 0.
For a Sergeant	2: 6.
For a Corporal	2: 0.
For a Drummer	2: 0.
For a Fifer	2: 0.
For a Scout	5: 0.
For a Private	1: 6.

Finally all the claims were adjusted. To follow this in detail, would prove interesting, but require far too much space. Suffice it to say that Lord Dunmore's War in 1774, cost Virginia, in her Colonial currency, the sum of £350,000 :00 :0.

---

8. Hening's "Statutes at Large," Vol. IX., p. 61, 62.

THE POINT PLEASANT BATTLE MONUMENT.

Twenty-two feet square at the base and eighty-six feet in height. The plinths and obelisk are constructed of Balfour Granite from quarries near Salisbury, North Carolina; the statue thereon being made of Westerly Granite from Rhode Island.

CHAPTER IX.

*The Battlefield Unmarked—Steps Leading to the Erection of a Battle
Monument—Description of the Same.*

The day after the battle of Point Pleasant, Colonel Christian's
Fincastle men who had arrived at eleven o'clock the preceding evening, collected the dead who were buried without the pomp of war.
"This day," says Colonel Fleming, "were buried the men who were
slain yesterday and died last night, in different burying places, and
the following officers and Gentlemen in the Magazine: To-wit, Colonel Charles Lewis, Colonel John Field, Captain John Murray, with
his half brother, George Cameron, Captain Robert McClennahan, Captain Samuel Wilson, Lieutenant Hugh Allen and Mr. John Frogg."[1]
It was a heap of slain, and here they lay for many years, on a
neglected battle plain. Early travelers expressed regret because of
this.

Stephen T. Mitchell, editor of *The Spirit of the Old Dominion,*
was on the field at Point Pleasant in 1827—fifty-two years after the
battle, and at that time wrote as follows:

"I have often passed the tombs of those who fell that fatal day; and,
frequently, upon the mild summer's evening, have I strayed over the
open common which was the battle ground. Fifty years have elapsed,
and the remains of the gallant Lewis and his officers, are yet suffered to
moulder within the unhallowed precincts of a stable yard. No index
save vague rumor guides the curious traveller to their graves; no sculp-
tured marble, no plain monument reminds the free born of Virginia, that
on this ground the gallantry of his fore-fathers led them to a bloody but
glorious death."[2]

RESOLUTIONS IN THE VIRGINIA ASSEMBLY:—On the 10th of March,
1849, Hon. James M. Laidley, a member of the Virginia House of

---

1. "Documentary History of Dunmore's War." p. 345.
2. See *Spirit of the Old Dominion*, Vol. I., No. 3, p. 155.

Delegates from the Kanawha-Putnam Delegate District, submitted the following Preamble and Resolutions relative to a Battle Monument at Point Pleasant:

WHEREAS: It has been a time honored custom to perpetuate, in an enduring form, a people's gratitude to those who have signalized themselves by deeds of patriotic heroism: And whereas, it is meet and proper that the people of Virginia shall commemorate, in a suitable manner, the bravery of her sons who nobly fell at Point Pleasant in the defense of the soil which has since become the home of a peaceful, flourishing and happy people:

1. Be it therefore resolved, by the General Assembly of Virginia, that a grateful tribute to the memory of her gallant citizens who fell on the tenth day of October, seventeen hundred and seventy-four, in the battle which was fought near the mouth of the Great Kanawha river, between the Virginia forces, under command of Gen. Andrew Lewis, and the confederated tribes of Shawnee, Delaware, Mingo and Cayuga Indians, a plain, substantial monument, with appropriate inscriptions, shall be erected at or near the scene of said battle.

2. Resolved, That Charles Clendennin and Thomas Lewis, of Mason county; John D. Lewis, of Kanawha county; Samuel H. Lewis, of Rockinham county; Rice D. Montague, of Montgomery county; Madison Pitser, of Roanoke county; Rufus Pitser, of Botetourt county; James A. Cochran, of Augusta county; Robert G. Ward, of Culpeper county; Milton Kirtley, of Madison county, and Thomas Creigh, of Greenbrier county, be, and they are hereby appointed collectors, to receive donations to aid in the execution of the purpose hereby declared.

3. Resolved, That George W. Summers, of Kanawha county; and Charles Clendennin and Peter H. Steenbergen, of Mason county, be, and they are hereby appointed commissioners to design said monument, and to direct what inscriptions shall be placed thereon; and also to contract for and superintend the erection of the same, and to take all necessary measures for the proper execution of the work. And the General Assembly hereby pledge the faith of the State that when a sum not less than $—— thousand dollars has been contributed by individuals for the construction of said monument, a sum not exceeding $—— thousand dollars shall be appropriated by the General Assembly in the aid of the same.[3]

On motion of Mr. Laidley, this was laid on the table and ordered printed. No further action was taken thereon.

POINT PLEASANT MONUMENT ASSOCIATION CREATED:—Years passed by with nothing done, but finally on the first day of April,

---

3. See Pub. Doc. No. 82, session of the General Assembly of Virginia, 1848-49.

1860, the General Assembly passed an act to incorporate the "Point Pleasant Monument Association."[4]

This provided that Mrs. John S. Lewis, Miss Ellen Steenbergen, and Miss Elizabeth Smith, all of Mason county, (now West Virginia) together with such others as might be associated with them, be made a body politic and corporate, with authority to purchase land and erect a monument on the battlefield of Point Pleasant. But action was soon stayed. The Civil War was at hand, and when that storm had passed away, a new Commonwealth—West Virginia—had arisen on the western slope of the Alleghenies, and in it lay the battlefield of Point Pleasant with its story of historic achievement.

A CENTENNIAL CELEBRATION:—Saturday, October 10, 1874, was the Centennial Anniversary of the battle at Point Pleasant, and the day was fittingly observed. Dr. Samuel G. Shaw was President of the Centennial Society under the auspices of which the exercises were held.   Francis A. Guthrie, Attorney-at-Law was the chairman of the committee on arrangements. The morning was dark and gloomy, but soon the sun broke forth and ushered in a beautiful autumn day. A large procession was formed on Main Street and marched to the Mason County Fair Grounds. In the line were a company of Cadets from the West Virginia University; an Artillery Company from Gallipolis, Ohio, and the Knights of Pythias, a splendid body of men, from that place. The music was furnished by the Drum Corps with the Cadets; the Constalk Brass Band of Point Pleasant, and a Brass Band from Ravenswood. On the Grand Stand at the Fair Grounds. were, among others, Dr. S. G. Shaw, Dr. Andrew R. Barbee, of Point Pleasant, together with Hon. George C. Sturgiss of Morgantown; Dr. Thomas Creigh, of Greenbrier county; and Colonel Lewis Ruffner and Hon. Benjamin H. Smith, of Charleston, the latter the orator of the day. Addresses were also made by Hon. Henry S. Walker, Dr. Creigh and Mr. Sturgiss. Then Rev. William E. Hill offered the following preamble and resolution which was unanimously adopted:

WHEREAS: The battle of Point Pleasant has hastened the material prosperity of this and other states by the sacrifice of noble blood:—

1. Therefore, be it Resolved, That a committee of three with power to

---

4. See acts of the General Assembly of Virginia 1859-60, p. 576.

engage others, be appointed to solicit contributions for the purpose of erecting a monument and purchasing the ground around about the spot where the remains of our heroes now repose:

2. That this committee be empowered to raise a subscription on the ground today; to write to the descendants of the brave men who were engaged in, or fell on the field at Point Pleasant; asking them to aid in this work by contribution; to ask the Legislature of Virginia, West Virginia, Kentucky, and Ohio to make appropriations to this work and to request also the Congress of the United States to make an appropriation to the same end.

Dr. Shaw, the president, then appointed as a soliciting committee, Rev. William E. Hill, Dr. William P. Neal, Dr. Charles T. B. Moore, and it raised by subscription about six hundred dollars that day.

In the evening the procession was re-formed and took up the line of march from the Fair Grounds to the town, where, at the head of Viand Street, the column received the hearse and casket containing the bones of some of the heroes who fell in the battle, they having been exhumed the preceding day. Here the cadets, with reversed arms and muffled drums, took their position as an escort and the column moved to the point of land where once stood old Fort Randolph, and where the remains were re-interred with military honors. During this time the church bells of the town were tolled and minute guns fired by the Artillery Company. The beautiful Burial Service of the Church was read; a benediction pronounced, and thus ended the first Centennial celebration of the battle of Point Pleasant.[5]

FIRST APPROPRIATION FOR A MONUMENT:—The interest and patriotism aroused on that centennial day never entirely ceased. Application was made to the Legislature of the new State of West Virginia the next year, and that body appropriated the sum "of $3,500.00 to aid in the purchase of land and the erection of a monument in commemoration of the battle of Point Pleasant." This was approved by Governor John J. Jacob, February 25, 1875.[6]

This money was drawn from the State Treasury, but before it was expended, the Legislature on the 6th of December, 1875, adopted Joint Resolution No. 24.[7] In which it was declared that:

"The battle of Point Pleasant was an event of deep and enduring inter-

5. See the *Weekly Register*, printed at Point Pleasant, October 15, 1874.
6. See acts of West Virginia, 1875, pp. 29-30.
7. See acts of 1875, p. 245.

est, exhibiting in a remarkable degree the courage and patriotism of the early settlers of our country; that an event so distinguished in our history should be commemorated by a monument to be erected upon the spot where those gallant defenders sacrificed their lives, and where their sacred remains now lie buried."

Then it was stated that West Virginia had already made an appropriation from her treasury for this purpose and it was resolved that the Governor be requested to communicate with those of Virginia, Ohio, and Kentucky, and solicit aid from their states in the erection of the monument. In addition to this, the Senators and Representatives of these states were requested to co-operate with those from West Virginia in their efforts to secure aid from the National Government for this purpose. The persons who had drawn the money from the State Treasury now decided to await in anticipation of further appropriations, and invested the sum in hand at a good rate of interest.

LEGISLATIVE ACTION IN 1897:—Thus matters continued for twenty-one years, in all of which no additional aid was received, and on the 26th of February, 1897, the State Legislature adopted House Joint Resolution No. 34,[8] in which it was set forth that:

The money which had been appropriated in 1875, to aid in the purchasing of land and erecting a monument at Point Pleasant, had never been expended for that purpose; and the Governor was authorized to appoint three trustees to carry into effect the act making that appropriation.

In compliance therewith Governor George W. Atkinson appointed Judge John W. English, Dr. Andrew R. Barbee, and Judge Francis A. Guthrie, trustees. But these gentlemen found the money invested for a specified time, therefore not available, and they were unable to accomplish anything.

LEGISLATIVE ACTION IN 1901:—Four more years passed away, and on February 7th, 1901, the Legislature adopted Resolution No. 12, which declared it to be the duty of the Legislature to carry into effect the object of the appropriation of 1875, for a monument at Point Pleasant and directing the Governor to appoint three trustees for this purpose.

THE TRUSTEES APPOINTED—WORK BEGUN:—In compliance with

---

8. See acts of of West Virginia, 1897, p. 278.

this resolution, Governor Albert B. White, did, on the 29th day of March, 1901, appoint as such trustees for the purpose aforesaid John P. Austin, of Redmond; Virgil A. Lewis, of Mason City; Charles C. Bowyer, of Point Pleasant, all of Mason county. As such they qualified April 18, 1901, and entered into a personal bond jointly in the penalty of $10,000.00 which was approved by the County Court of Mason county. May 25th ensuing, they affected an organization by electing Mr. Austin, President; Mr. Lewis, Secretary; and Mr. Bowyer, Treasurer. On the 13th of July, 1901, they received from the former trustees the sum of $8,788.33, this being the amount of the appropriation of 1875, together with accrued interest, the fund having more than doubled itself in the twenty-six years of its investment. Further, the trustees were informed that there were in the hands of Mr. Peter S. Lewis, Treasurer of the Ladies Monument Association the sum of $2,007.84, which amount had been contributed by individuals to aid in the erection of a monument. The land selected for this, is the square at the apex of the angle formed by the confluence of the two rivers—the Ohio and Great Kanawha—on which the Virginian army was encamped at the beginning of the battle, and where its honored dead who fell in the contest, were buried. This is high land and contains about two and one half acres. It had been laid out in lots, and from the owners, the trustees bought and paid for these, as follows:

To Thomas J. Darst, $550.00; to J. H. Stone, and others $3,000.00; to John D. McCulloch, $1,000.00; to Nancy A. Varian and others, $1,200.00; and to R. A. Comstock, $2,250.00—a total of $8,000.00.

For these properties deeds were properly executed, vesting title in the State of West Virginia, and were recorded in the office of the clerk of the County Court of Mason county. The Legislature in 1905, made an appropriation of $5,000.00 to aid in the erection of the monument.

AID FROM CONGRESS:—Hon. Charles E. Hogg, of Mason county, while a member of the Fiftieth Congress introduced a bill carrying with it an appropriation to aid in the erection of a Battle Monument at Point Pleasant, but this failed of passage. Imbued with the idea, of the National character of the battle, the trustees, in February

1902, went to Washington, where the State's entire Delegation— Senators and Representatives—urged upon Congress an appropriation for the purpose desired. Annually for six years, the trustees kept the matter before that body and at length, in 1908, the sum of $10,000.00 was appropriated to be expended under the direction and approval of the Secretary of War, in aid of and for the erection of the monument. The trustees feeling that at last they had a sufficient sum with which to erect a suitable structure, took steps to do this. In August, 1908, they proceeded to Washington where they had an interview with Hon. Luke E. Wright, Secretary of War. He requested a map of grounds showing elevation and other data, and evidence as to right of way thereto. Captain William H. Howard, a Civil Engineer of Point Pleasant, made the map, and Colonel Hiram R. Howard, mayor of the town, made official statement as to the streets leading to the site on which the monument was to be erected. On the 21st day of October, ensuing, the trustees had a second interview with Secretary Wright, who approved plans, they having been previously approved by Governor William M. O. Dawson. They then requested government supervision in the erection of the monument, and this was referred to Captain A. F. Alstaetter of the War Department, who was stationed at Wheeling. The Van Amringe Granite Company, of Boston, Massachusetts, which had erected many monuments at Gettysburg and on other fields, furnished plans and specifications, which were accepted, and a contract awarded it at a meeting at the office of Captain Alstætter, in Wheeling, December 14th, 1908. These people employed Charles Frederick Hess, of Point Pleasant, to put in the concrete foundation at the center of *Tu-enda-wee Park,*[9]

9. TU-ENDA-WEE PARK—This is a name bestowed, in 1901, upon the square on which the monument has ben erected. In that year the writer was engaged in some research work relative to Indian geographical names in West Virginia. Among numerous other works he consulted the "Glossary of Indian Names," prepared by Colonel John Johnston, who was the Government Indian Agent at Upper Piqua, Ohio, for fifty years. In the list of Wyandot terms, he found that of *Tu-enda-wee,* signifying a "triangular point of land at the confluence of rivers," not a particular point at any particular place, but a kind of common noun, applicable to any one of a class or kind. He spoke of this at the time to members of the Charles Lewis Chapter of the Daughters of the American Revolution, at Point Pleasant. These suggested at once that it would be a good name for the battle park at that place; and it was due to their suggestion that it was thus named. That was but eight years ago, but in that time, it has been stated that it is a Shawnee term; that it signifies the mingling of waters; and it has been misspelled almost as many times as it has been used. The truth is that it is a Wyandot term; that it means a triangular point of land; and its proper spelling is *Tu-enda-wee*—pronounced as if spelled *Too-endy-wee.*

as designated by Captain William H. Howard. This he began on the 11th day of May, 1909, when ground was broken by Daniel Crump Wartenburg, an employee of Mr. Hess. The large mass of human bones—the remains of those who fell in battle—which were removed from the excavation, were carefully placed in a box and re-interred by Captain Hess under the northeast corner of the monument, there ultimately to mingle with mother earth. James E. Amedon, of Manchester Depot, Vermont, arrived May 23rd, and assumed the supervision of construction. His stone or granite "setter" was John Kernehan, of Adams, Massachusetts; the "rigger," the man in charge of the derrick, being Herman Kappes, of Gettysburg, Pennsylvania. The first car load of granite arrived at Point Pleasant, June 1st., from the quarries of the Balfour Pink Granite Company, which is distant five miles from the town of Salisbury, North Carolina, it being shipped by the Southern Railroad, and the first block thereof was set in place on the 14 of the same month. At 11:30 P. M. Thursday, July 22nd., the upper part of the derrick, standing 105 feet above the surface was struck by lightning and badly damaged, but the monument, then but thirty feet high, was uninjured. The capstone was put in place at 11:10 a. m. Monday, August 22nd, 1909, when the structure was completed. It is twenty-two feet square at the base; eighty-six feet high; and contains one hundred and fifty-two granite blocks, the whole weighing one hundred and forty-three tons. The statue, facing the east, standing eight feet high, and weighing two tons, is cut of Westerly Granite, by the Smith Granite Company, of Westerly, Rhode Island. The bronze panels and bas-relief were cast by Albert Russell & Sons Company, of Newburyport, Massachusetts, the historical data thereon having been compiled by Virgil A. Lewis, in compliance with an order of the trustees. At last, one hundred and thirty-five years thereafter, the National Government and that of the State of West Virginia, acting jointly, have properly marked the spot on which was waged the most desperate as well as the most important battle ever fought between the White men and Indians in America.

CHAPTER X.

As a boy residing near the battlefield of Point Pleasant, the author heard the oft repeated stories of how Captain Michael Cresap had, in cold blood, murdered the relatives of Logan, the Mingo chieftain; how Lord Dunmore had, in 1774, encouraged the Indians to wage war against the frontier for the purpose of distracting the attention of the Virginians from the complications between the Colonies and the Mother Country, then pending, and how he had delayed the march of the Northern Division of the army commanded by himself, that the Southern Division under General Lewis, might be destroyed at Point Pleasant; and that therefore, that battle was the first of the Revolution; and how General Lewis, on meeting Lord Dunmore on the Pickaway Plains, had disobeyed the orders of the Governor, by continuing to advance, after receiving orders to halt his army. Later, he read one or more of these statements in the writing of Joseph Dodridge, published in 1824; of Hugh Paul Taylor, in 1829; of Alexander Scott Withers, 1831; and of others who followed them, and assuming that these authors had followed unimpeachable authority for the statements they made, instead of vague traditions, he, himself, years ago, when writing of the Border Wars, believed and accepted their statements, as history. Since then he has had the opportunity of examining a great mass of contemporary documents relating to Dunmore's War, which have been collected and rendered available to all students who desire to consult original sources of information. A careful examination of these reveals incontrovertable proof of the innocence of Captain Cresap; of the honesty of purpose and faithfulness of Lord Dunmore to the interests of the people of Virginia; and of the soldierly qualities of General Lewis, who did not disobey the orders of his superior officer, in front of an enemy on the Pickaway Plains.

Because Captain Michael Cresap was the most prominent man in the vicinity of Wheeling, at the time Logan's people were killed, it was but natural that this chieftian should suspect him of committing the barbarous act. Of this he had no proof, but in his speech delivered to Captain John Gibson at the treaty of Camp Charlotte, he preferred the charge against Cresap therein, as the perpetrator of the bloody deed. At the time, Captain Gibson assured him that Cresap was entirely innocent of it. Within the next few years affidavits testifying to this, were made by Ebenezer Zane, the founder of Wheeling; Charles Polk at whose house on Cross creek, now in Brooke county, West Virginia, Daniel Greathouse assembled the men who perpetrated the horrid deed; by William Robinson, who was taken prisoner by Logan July 12, 1774, on the West Fork of the Monogahela river, about two miles from Clarksburg, now Harrison county, West Virginia; by Joshua Baker at whose house the Indians were killed; and by John Sappington who was one of the men with Greathouse; and all printed in the appendix to Jefferson's "Notes on Virginia." And further: The letter[1] written by General George Rogers Clark, June 17, 1798, to Doctor Samuel Brown, this being now among the "Jefferson Papers," in the Department of State at Washington. In it he stated that he was at Wheeling at the time Logan's people were killed; that he was personally acquainted with Captain Cresap; and that he was in no wise connected with the barbarous act; that he (Cresap) was violently opposed to it; that he left Wheeling to go to Redstone on the Monongahela river, two days before it was committed; and that it was the work of Daniel Greathouse and party. Yet in the face of all this evidence, some of the writers of the Border Wars have been for a hundred years repeating the story and connecting with it the name of Captain Michael Cresap, a brave soldier of the Revolution who lost his life in the struggle for American Independence. Certainly, no one who had made proper investigation of the subject would do this.

THE ALLEGED TREACHERY OF LORD DUNMORE:—Let us make a calm and unprejudiced enquiry, regarding this, and in doing so, use only competent witnesses and contemporary documents relating to Dunmore's War. We know of his part therein; so it will be needless to further consider that. He criticized the House of Burgesses for

---

1. Printed in English's "Conquest of the Northwest," Vol. II., p. 1029.

authorizing him to prosecute the war, and then adjourning without providing for its exigencies. He gave assurance to the messengers who bore to Williamsburg, tidings of the savage atrocities that he would not only supply the border men with ammunition, at his own risk; but, that he would furnish men for the defence of the frontier."[10]

Under date of June 8th, 1774, Captain Valentine Crawford, of Frederick county, Virginia, then at Jacobs' creek, on the Yohogany river, wrote Colonel George Washington regarding the distressed condition of the frontier and said: "But it is a happy circumstance for us that Lord Dunmore is so warm in our favor."[11]

Colonel William Preston in his Circular Letter of July 20, 1774, addressed to the Fincastle men, urging them to enlist for the defence of the frontier settlements, said:—"The Earl of Dunmore is deeply engaged in it. The House of Burgesses will no doubt enable his Lordship to reward every Volunteer in a handsome manner."[12]

From Winchester in Frederick county, Virginia, under date of Sunday, August 14th, Lord Dunmore then engaged in organizing the Northern Division of the Army, wrote William, Earl of Dartmouth, the British Secretary of State for the American Colonies, and said:—

"The Shawnees, Mingoes, and some of the Delewares, have fallen on our frontiers, and killed, scalped, and most cruelly murdered a great many of our men, women and children * * * * I hope in eight or ten days to march with a body of men over the Allegheny mountains, and then down the Ohio, to the mouth of the Scioto, and if I can possibly fall upon these lower towns undiscovered, I think I shall be able to put an end to this cruel war."[13]

If there were no other evidence extant, this letter should exonerate Dunmore from the charge of a betrayal of the Virginia people.

Let us continue this examination of contemporary documents relating to Dunmore's War, and thus learn of the estimation in which he was held by those who served under him, as well as other representative Virginians who were otherwise associated with him. The Northern Division of the Army, homeward bound from Camp Charlotte, halted at Fort Gower, at which place the officers assembled and gave expression to the following:

---

10. "The Washington-Crawford Letters," p. 90.
11. "The Washington-Crawford Letters," p. 90.
12. "Documentary History of Dunmore's War," p. 92.
13. "Documentary History of Dunmore's War." p. 151.

A RESOLUTION BY THE OFFICERS, WHO SERVED UNDER LORD DUNMORE,
ADOPTED AT FORT GOWER, MOUTH OF HOCKHOCKING
RIVER, NOVEMBER 5, 1774.

"*Resolved*, That we entertain the greatest respect for his Excellency the
Right Honourable Lord *Dunmore*, who commanded the expedition against
the *Shawanese;* and who, we are confident underwent the great fatigue of
this singular campaign from no other motive than the true interest of this
country.
Signed by order and in behalf of the whole Corps,

BENJAMIN ASHBY, *Clerk*."[14]

Among these officers were Colonel William Crawford, and Colonel
Adam Stephen, both General officers in the war for Independence;
and Captain Daniel Morgan, afterward General Morgan, likewise of
the Revolution; Captain George Rogers Clark, later the Conqueror
of the Illinois Country; and many others afterward prominent in
military life.

Lord Dunmore returned to Williamsburg, on Sunday, December 4th,
having been absent one hundred and fifty days, and found that an
interesting event had occurred in his family. Just twenty-four hours
before his arrival, there was the birth of a daughter who received the
name of Virginia, in honor of the Colony in which the father was the
executive head.[15] On the next day, December 5th he was the recipient
of the following:

ADDRESS OF THE CITIZENS OF THE CITY OF WILLIAMSBURG, DECEMBER
5, 1774, TO JOHN, EARL OF DUNMORE.

"To his Excellency the Right Honourable John, Earl of Dunmore,
his Majesty's Lieutenant and Governor-General of the Colony and
Dominion of Virginia, and Vice Admiral of the Same.

MY LORD:—We his Majesty's most dutiful and loyal subjects, the Mayor,
Recorder, Aldermen, and Common Council, of the city of *Williamsburg*,
in Common Hall assembled, beg leave to embrace the earliest opportunity
of congratulating your Lordship on the conclusion of a dangerous and
fatiguing service in which you have lately been engaged, and on your
return to this City.
It is with pleasure we hear your Lordship has been able to defeat the

---

14. "American Archives," Fourth Series, Vol. I., pp. 962, 963.
15. See "Last Journal of Horace Walpole," Vol. I., p. 492.

designs of a cruel and insidious enemy, and at the same time that your Lordship has escaped those dangers to which your person must have been frequently exposed.

Permit us also upon this occasion, to express our congratulations on the addition to your family by the birth of a daughter; and to assure you that we wish to your Lordship every degree of felicity, and that we shall contribute towards its attainment, as far as lies in our power, during your residence among us."[16]

THE REPLY OF LORD DUNMORE TO THE CITIZENS OF WILLIAMSBURG.

To the above Address, his Excellency was pleased to return the following Answer:

"GENTLEMEN:—I am obliged to you for the Address. The fatigue and danger of the service which I undertook, out of commiseration for the deplorable state which, in particular, the back inhabitants were in, and to manifest my solicitude for the saffety of the country in general, which his Majesty has committed to my care, has been amply rewarded by the satisfaction I feel in having been able to put an effectual stop to a bloody war.

I thank you for the notice you are pleased to take of the event which has happened in my family; and, I doubt not that, as I have hitherto experienced the marks of your civility, you will continue in the same friendly disposition toward me."[16]

William and Mary College at Williamsburg, founded in 1692, is the oldest institution of its kind south of the Potomac river. In it at this time two of Lord Dunmore's sons, George and Alexander, were students. How the President and Faculty of the College extended a welcome to the Governor on his return from the Indian Expedition is shown by the following:

ADDRESS OF THE PRESIDENT AND PROFESSORS OF WILLIAM AND MARY
COLLEGE TO JOHN, EARL OF DUNMORE.

To his Excellency, the Earl of DUNMORE, Governor of VIRGINIA.
May it please your Excellency:
We his Majesty's dutiful and loyal subjects, the President and Professors of William and Mary College, moved by an impulse of unfeigned joy, cannot help congratulating your Excellency on such a series of agreeable events, as the success of your enterprise against the Indians, the

---

16. "American Archives," Fourth Series, Vol. 1., pp. 1018-19.

addition to your family by the birth of a daughter, and your safe as well as glorious return to the capital of this Dominion.

May the great fatigues and dangers which you so readily and cheerfully underwent in the service of your Government, be ever crowned with victory! May you ever find the publick benefits thence arising attended with domestic blessings! And, may you always feel the enlivening pleasure of reading in the countenances around you, wherever you turn your eyes, such expressions of affection as can be derived only from applauding and grateful hearts!"[17]

To which his Excellency was pleased to return the following answer:

THE REPLY OF LORD DUNMORE TO THE PRESIDENT AND FACULTY OF WILLIAM AND MARY COLLEGE.

"GENTLEMEN:—I cannot but receive every instance of the attention of a learned and respectable body, such as yours, with a great degree of satisfaction; but the affectionate and very obliging terms in which you are pleased to express your good wishes towards me, on this occasion, demand my cordinal thanks, and will ever be impressed on my mind."[17]

Away down on the sea coast was the borough of Norfolk overlooking historic Hampton Roads. Intelligence of the return of the Governor from his western expedition speedily reached the old town, and its officials took the following action:—

ADDRESS OF THE MAYOR, RECORDER, ALDERMAN, AND COMMON COUNCIL OF THE BOROUGH OF NORFOLK, TO JOHN, EARL OF DUNMORE.

To the Right Honourable JOHN, Earl of DUNMORE, his Majesty's Lieutenant and Governor-General of the Colony and Dominion of Virginia, and Vice Admiral of the Same.

"MY LORD:—We his Majesty's most dutiful and loyal subjects, the Mayor, Recorder, Aldermen, and Common Council of the Borough of Norfolk in Common Hall assembled, impressed with a deep and grateful sense of the important services rendered to this Colony by your Excellency's seasonable and vigorous exertion in the late expedition against a deceitful and treacherous enemy, conducted under your auspices to so fortunate an issue, beg leave, by this testimony of our general respect, to congratulate your Excellency on the Happy event, and on your safe arrival at the capital.

While we applaud your Lordship's moderation in giving peace to a merciless foe, we cannot but exult in the happiness of our fellow-sub-

---

17. "American Archives" Fourth Series, Vol. I., p. 1019.

jects on the Frontiers, who, by your unremitted zeal and spirited conduct, have acquired the blessings of ease, security, and domestick enjoyment.

As we sincerely participate in every circumstance of your publick glory, neither can we be insensible of your private happiness in the birth of a daughter, and the recovery of Lady Dunmore, on which joyful occasion we beg leave also to add our most cordial congratulations; and we devoutly wish that, to the pleasing rememberance of having faithfully discharged your important trust of Government, you may have superadded the approbation of your Royal Master, the grateful returns of an happy people, and the honor of these distinctions reflected on a numerous and flourishing family."[18]

THE REPLY OF LORD DUNMORE.

"The Address of the Mayor, Recorder, Aldermen, and Common Council of the Borough of Norfolk, expressive of their duty and loyalty to the King, cannot but be extremely acceptable to me.

His Majesty, in his tender solicitude for the safety of his subjects, so lately exposed to the calamities of an Indian war, having signified his full approbation of the measures which I at first adopted for their relief, and as the issue of that event, the only circumstance of it of which he could not yet be informed, will entirely remove the paternal anxiety which he suffered on the occasion, I already enjoy, and have good reason to expect the continuance of one part of that high recompense which the gentlemen of the Borough of Norfolk have so kindly wished me, and the applause which they are pleased to bestow upon me greatly contributes toward another part, which is my ardent ambition to merit.

The notice which they take of my private concerns is obliging, as their approbation of my publick conduct is honorable to me, and both demand my most cordial thanks."[18]

The Council of State of the Colony of Virginia occupied to the House of Burgesses, the relation of a Senate. It consisted of twelve members, who were the advisors of the Governor. They likewise extended greetings and a welcome home, from the Ohio Wilderness.

ADDRESS OF THE COUNCIL OF STATE OF VIRGINIA, TO JOHN, EARL OF DUNMORE.

To the Right Honourable JOHN, Earl of DUNMORE, his Majesty's Lieutenant and Governor-General of the Colony and Dominion of VIRGINIA, and Vice-Admiral of the Same:

"MY LORD:—We, his Majesty's dutiful and loyal subjects, the Council

18. "American Archives," Fourth Series, Vol. I., pp. 1019-20.

of Virginia, with the most heartfelt joy and unfeigned pleasure, beg leave to offer our congratulations to your Lordship on your safe return, after the fatigues and dangers of a trublesome expedition.

Your Lordship's vigorous opposition to the incursions and ravages of an Indian enemy, hath effectually prevented the desolation of a growing back country, and the horrours of human carnage. The scene of war was remote from us; our properties and estates were not immediately exposed to the miseries consequent thereon; but though not equally interested, we sensibly participate in the blessings that are derived to our fellow-subjects in that quarter of the Colony, from the prospect of a permanent peace. The lenity you exercised towards the Indians, when they expected the cruelty of the victor, hath attached them to you from principle; and unless the intrigues of Traders, or the insidious arts of the enemies to this Government, should again foment differences, we flatter ourselves the present tranquility will not speedily be interrupted. You have taught them a lesson to which the savage breast was a stranger to—that clemency and mercy are not incompatible with power; and that havock and bloodshed are not the inseparable concomitants of success and victory.

Permit us, my Lord, to express our lively satisfaction at the addition to your family, by the birth of a daughter, and to assure you it is greatly heightened by the promising hopes the your Lady's recovery will be unattended with danger. We should be wanting in respect to her Ladyship, to omit any opportunity of testifying our esteem for her; an esteem that her exemplary piety and true dignity of conduct will ever command."[19]

To which his Excellency was pleased to return the following answer:

THE REPLY OF LORD DUNMORE.

"GENTLEMEN:—I am in the most sensible manner obliged to you for this Address. The motives which induced me to exert my efforts to relieve the back country from the calamity under which it lately laboured, would have been disappointed in one of their principal ends, if it had not met your approbation; and this very honourable testimony which you are now pleased to give me of it, conveys the highest gratification to me.

The cordiality of your expressions on the occasion of the addition to my family, and the distinguishing mark of the notice which you so kindly take of Lady Dunmore, attaches me to you by the strongest ties of gratitude and the warmest affection."[19]

---

19. "American Archives," Fourth Series, Vol., I., pp. 1043-1044.

RESOLUTION ADOPTED BY THE VIRGINIA CONVENTION WHICH ASSEM-
BLED AT RICHMOND, MARCH 20, 1775.

On the 20th day of March, 1775, one of the most important con-
ventions, the proceedings of which are recorded in the annals of Virginia, assembled in the town of Richmond.   On the fifth day of the
session, this body adopted, among others, the following Resolution:—

"*Resolved Unanimously*, That the most cordial thanks of the people of
this Colony are a tribute justly due to our worthy Governour, Lord
Dunmore, for his truly noble, wise, and spirited conduct on the late
expedition against our Indian enemy; a conduct which at once evinces his
Excellency's attention to the true interests of this Colony, and a zeal in
the Executive Department which no dangers can divert or difficulties
hinder from achieving the most important services to the people who
have the happiness to live under his administration."[20]

Among the members of that Convention who had served in Dunmore's War, were Colonel William Christian, of Fincastle; Captain
James Mercer, of Hampshire county; Captain Samuel McDowell,
of Augusta County; General Andrew Lewis and Lieutenant John
Bowyer, of Botetourt county; General Adam Stephen and Colonel
Robert Rutherford, of Berkeley county; and Captain John Neville
and John Harvie, of the "District of West Augusta."   Every one
of these men voted for the above Resolution, for the Journal states
that it was adopted *unanimously*.   Does any one think that if there
had been the least suspicion of treachery on the part of Dunmore
in that war, that these men, or any one of them would have voted in
favor of that resolution?   There too, sat Colonel George Washington,
a delegate from Fairfax county, the military genius of his time; he
too voted for the Resolution.   Would he have done this, had he
thought there had been dishonor on the part of Dunmore?

Of all the contemporary Documents which throw light on Dunmore's War none is of greater value than the following: Colonel
Christian's Fincastle men were heroes in that war, many of them were
among the killed and wounded at Point Pleasant; and the survivors
on that April day, 1775—the year following the war—assembled
in convention, and voiced the public sentiment of that time regarding
Lord Dunmore.

---

20. Journal of this Convention in "American Archives," Vol. II., pp. 165-170.

ADDRESS OF FREEHOLDERS OF FINCASTLE COUNTY (VIRGINIA) TO
LORD DUNMORE, APRIL 8, 1775.

To his Excellency the Right Honourable JOHN, Earl of DUN-
MORE, His Majesty's Lieutenant and Governor-General of the Colony of Virginia:

"MY LORD:—Notwithstanding the unhappy disputes that at present sub-
sist between the Mother Country and the Colonies, in which we have
given the publick our sentiments, yet justice and gratitude, as well
as a sense of our duty, induce us collectively to return your Lordship
our unfeigned thanks for the great services you have rendered the frontiers in general, and this county in particular, in the late expedition
against our enemy Indians.

In our former wars with the savages, we long suffered every species
of barbarity; many of our friends and fellow-subjects were inhumanly
butchered and carried into captivity, more to be dreaded than death itself; our houses plundered and burned and our country laid waste by an
enemy, against whom, from our dispersed situation, and their manner of
carrying on war, it was impossible to make a proper defence on our frontiers. Your Lordship being convinced of this, proposed to attack the
enemy in their own country, well judging that it would be the most effectual means to reduce them to reason, and be attended with little more
expense to the community than a partial defense of such an extensive
frontier. The proposal was cheerfully embraced, and the ardour of the
Militia to engage in that very necessary service, could only be equalled
by that of your Lordship in carrying it on. That the plan of an expedition should be laid when the season was far advanced, and near three
thousand choice troops raised in a few Counties, and put under the command of many brave and experienced Officers; that those forces should
be equipped and fully supplied with provisions, and march several hundred hundred miles through mountains to meet the enemy; that so many
Nations of warlike Indians should be reduced to sue for peace; that those
Troops should return victorious to their homes by the last of November;
and all this without any publick money in hand to defray any part of the
expense, shows at first view the immediate utility of the undertaking,
and must be a convincing proof that the Almighty, in a peculiar manner,
blessed our Lordship's attempts to establish peace, and stop the further
effusion of human blood; but that your Lordship should forego your ease,
and every domestick felicity, and march at the head of a body of those
Troops many hundred miles from the Seat of Government, cheerfully
undergoing all the fatigues of the campaign, by exposing your person, and
marching on foot with the officers and soldiers, commands our warmest

returns of gratitude; and the rather, as we have no instance of such con-descension in your Lordship's predecessors on any similar occasion.

We should be wanting in point of gratitude, were we to omit return-ing our thanks on this occasion to the Officers and Soldiers who entered into the service with so much alacrity. The memory of such as fell nobly fighting for their Country ought to be very dear to it.

That your Lordship may enjoy every domestic blessing; that you may long govern the brave and free people of Virginia, and that the present disturbances may be amicably settled, is the ardent wish of the inhabi-tants of Fincastle."[21]

THE REPLY OF LORD DUNMORE.

"I am very much obliged to the freeholders and inhabitants of the County of Fincastle for their Address, and am happy to find they think the service I undertook upon the occasion of the Indian disturbances merits their publick thanks. I assure them that they will ever find me equally ready to exert my best endeavours for every purpose which may tend to the security or promote the happiness of the people of VIR-GINIA."[21]

Major Angus McDonald, who commanded the preliminary expe-dition, and afterwards served under Dunmore in the Northern Divi-sion, writing Captain William Harrod, in January, 1775, says: "All the Country is well pleased with the Governor's Expedition."[22]

WHAT HISTORIANS SAY:—George Brancroft says, "Virginia has left on record her judgment, that Dunmore's conduct in this campaign, was truly noble, wise, and spirited."[23]

Theodore Roosevelt, speaking of the compliments paid Dunmore by the Virginians, adds, "And he fully deserved their gratitude."[24]

Consul W. Butterfield says:—"There can be no doubt of his Lord-ship's sincerity in taking these measures for protection of the fron-tiers; nor can there be any as to his acting in good faith toward Vir-ginia, in negotiating with the Indians the peace that followed."[25]

Reuben G. Thwaites says: "There seems to be no doubt that Dun-more was thoroughly in earnest; that he prosecuted the war with vigor and knew when to stop in order to secure the best terms."[26]

21. See "American Archives," Fourth Series, Vol. II., pp. 310_312.
22. See "Documentary History of Dunmore's War." p. 153.
23. See "History of the United States." Vol. IV., p. 88.
24. See "Winning of the West," Vol. I., p. 239.
25. See "The Washington-Crawford Letters," p. 90.
26. Note in Withers' "Chronicles of Border Warfare," p. 178.

The story of the treachery of Lord Dunmore is shown to have been an after thought—a thought originating after the Revolution—due to his adherance to his Home Government during that struggle.

DID GENERAL LEWIS DISOBEY ORDERS?:—The highest virtue of a soldier is his obediance to the orders of his superiors. The over-zealous friends of General Andrew Lewis have for a century done to his memory a great injustice, by asserting that when, on his arrival at the Pickaway Plains, he pressed on toward the Indian towns, after having received orders from Lord Dunmore to halt his army, because a treaty of peace was being negotiated with the Indians; also that there was bitter animosity between him and the Governor. Fortunately for the truth of history and the reputation of General Lewis, Captain John Stuart, the historian of the Southern Division of the army—he who had been in the thickest of the fight at Point Pleasant, and also in front of the line in the march through the Ohio Wilderness—was present at the meeting at Camp Charlotte, and here is his account of it:—

"Having finished our entrenchments (at Point Pleasant) and put every-thing in order for securing the wounded from danger after the battle, we crossed the Ohio river in our march to the Shawnee towns. Captain Arbuckle was our guide, who was equally esteemed as a soldier and a fine woodman. When we came to the prairie on Killicanic creek, we saw the smoke of a small Indian town, which was deserted and set on fire upon our approach. Here we met an express from the Governor's Camp, who had arrived near the nation and proposed peace with the Indians. The governor promised them that the war should be no further prosecuted, and that he would stop the march of Lewis' Army before any more hos-tilities should be committed upon them. The governor, therefore, with the White Fish] warrier, set off and met us at Killicanic creek, and then Colonel Lewis received his orders to return his army as he (the Governor) had proposed terms of peace with the Indians, which he (was) assured should be accomplished. His Lordship requested Colonel Lewis to intro-duce him to his officers; and we were accordingly ranged in rank, and had the honor of an introduction to the Governor and Commander-in-Chief, who politely thanked us for services rendered on so momentous an occasion, and assured us of his high esteem and respect for our conduct. On the Governor's consulting Colonel Lewis, it was deemed necessary that a garrison should be established at Point Pleasant, to intercept and prevent the Indians from crossing the Ohio to our side; as also to prevent any whites from crossing over to the side of the Indians."[27]

It can not be that these statements will continue to be made in the future as in the past. Original sources of information are now abundant, easily available, and research among these will supply proof that Captain Cresap was not the leader of the men who killed Chief Logan's relatives; that General Lewis was not so lost to the dignity and character of a true soldier, as to disobey the orders of his superior officer in the presence of an enemy; that Lord Dunmore was not guilty of double-dealing with the Virginians; that the Indians were not, in 1774, the allies of Great Britain, and that they did not become such, until the spring of 1778. Henceforth let there be accuracy of historic statement, and this will add to, rather than detract from the importance and glory of the victory won at the mouth of the Great Kanawha by the men of 1774—a victory won in a battle in which only Virginians and Indians were engaged.

---

27. See Stuart's "Memoirs of the Indian Wars and Other Occurrences," p. 57.

CHAPTER XI.

POETRY OF THE BATTLE OF POINT PLEASANT.

THE CAMP SONG AT POINT PLEASANT—THE SHAWNEE BATTLE ON THE
BANKS OF THE OHIO—THE BATTLE SONG OF THE GREAT KANA-
WHA—BATTLE OF POINT PLEASANT: A CENTENNIAL ODE.

Battles have been in all ages a favorite theme for the poets lay.
That of Point Pleasant has been thus commemorated in verse as
well as prose. The first of these productions appears in the Journal of Ensign James Newell, of Captain William Herbert's Company. He was wounded in the battle, but crossed the Ohio with
the Army, October 16th—six days thereafter. The following verses
appearing in his Journal, were written on the battlefield, or possibly
on the opposite bank of the Ohio:—

THE CAMP SONG AT POINT PLEASANT.

Bold Virginians all, each cheer up your heart.
We will see the Shawnees before that we part,
We will never desert, nor will we retreat,
Until that our Victory be quite complete.

Ye offspring of Britain! Come stain not you name
Nor forfeit your right to your forefathers' fame,
If the Shawnees will fight, we never will fly,
We'll fight & we'll conquer, or else we will die.

Great Dunmore our General valiant & Bold
Excells the great Heroes—the Heroes of old;
When he doth command we will always obey,
When he bids us fight, we will not run away.

Good Lewis our Colonel, courageous and Brave,
We wish too command us—our wish let us have.
In camp he is pleasant, in War he is bold
Appears like great Cæsar—great Cæsar of old.

Our Colonels & Captains commands we'll obey,
If the Shawnees should run we will bid them to stay,
Our Arms, they are Rifles, our men Volunteers
We'll fight & we'll conquer you need have no fears.

Come Gentlemen all, come strive to excel,
Strive not to shoot often, but strive to shoot well.
Each man like a Hero can make the woods ring,
And extend the Dominion of George our Great King.

Then to it, let's go with might & with main,
Tho' some that set forward return not again;
Let us quite lay aside all cowardly fear
In hope of returning before the new year.

The land it is good, it is just to our mind,
Each will have his part if his Lordship be kind.
The Ohio once ours, we'll live at our ease,
With a Bottle & glass to drink when we please.

Here's a health to King George & Charlotte his mate
Wishing our Victory may soon be complete
And a kind female friend along by our Side
In riches & splendor till Death to abide.

Health to great Dunmore our general also,
Wishing he may conquer wherever he go.
Health to his Lady—may they long happy be
And a health, my good friends, to you & to me.

———

When Henry Howe, the author of "Historical Collections of Virginia," was in Mason county, now West Virginia, in 1844, collecting data for his work, he visited a number of early settlers. Of one of these he writes as follows:—

"There is living on Thirteen-mile creek, Mr. Jesse Van Bibber, an aged pioneer of this county. His life, like his own mountain stream, was rough and turbulent at its commencement; but as it nears its

close, calm and peaceful, beautifully reflects the Christian virtues.
From conversation with him we gathered many interesting anecdotes
and incidents illustrating the history of this region. I wrote the
following down from his lips: It was made on the battle of Point
Pleasant, sometimes called 'The Shawnee Battle.' "

THE SHAWNEE BATTLE ON THE BANKS OF THE OHIO.

Let us mind the tenth of October,
Seventy-four which caused woe,
The Indian savages they did cover
The pleasant banks of the Ohio.

The battle beginning in the morning,
Throughout the day lasted sore,
Till the evening shades were turning down
Upon the banks of the Ohio.

Judgment proceeds to execution,
Let fame throughout all dangers go,
Our heroes fought with resolution
Upon the banks of the Ohio.

Seven score lay dead and wounded
Of champions that did face their foe,
By which the heathen were confounded,
Upon the banks of the Ohio.

Col. Lewis and some noble captains,
Did down to death like Uriah go,
Alas! their heads wound up in napkins,
Upon the banks of the Ohio.

Kings lamented their mighty fallen
Upon the mountains of Gilboa,
And now we mourn for brave Hugh Allen,
Far from the banks of the Ohio.

O bless the mighty King of Heaven
For all his wonderous works below,
Who hath to us the victory given,
Upon the banks of the Ohio.

The manuscript of the following poem was sent to Dr. Lyman C. Draper, in 1845, by Charles H. Lewis of Staunton, Virginia, with the statement that he had found it on one of the lids of his grand-mother's Bible. It is published in the "Documentary History of Dunmore's War," pp. 436, 437, it being printed from the manuscript in the 'Draper Collection' in the Library of the State Historical Society of Wisconsin.

THE BATTLE SONG OF THE GREAT KANAWHA.

Ye daughters and sons of Virginia incline
Your ears to a story of woe;
I sing of a time when your fathers and mine
Fought for us on the Ohio.

In seventeen hundred and seventy four,
The month of October, we know,
An army of Indians, two thousand or more,
Encamped on the Ohio.

The Shawnees, Wyandotes and Delawares, too,
As well as the tribe of Mingoe,
Invaded our lands, and our citizens slew,
On the south of the Ohio.

Andrew Lewis the gallant, and Charlie the brave,
With Mathews and Fleming also,
Collected an army, our country to save,
On the banks of the Ohio.

With Christian, and Shelby, and Elliot, and Paul.
And Stuart and Arbuckle and Crow
And soldiers one thousand and ninety in all
They marched to the Ohio.

These sons of the mountains renowned of old
All volunteered freely to go
And conquer their foeman, like patriots bold,
Or fall by the Ohio.

They marched thro' the untrodden wilds of the west,
O'er mountains and rivers also,
And halted, at Point Pleasant, their bodies to rest,
On the banks of the Ohio.

The Army of Indians in battle array,
Under Cornstalk and Ellinipsico,
Was met by the forces of Lewis that day,
On the banks of the Ohio.

They brought on the battle at breaking of day,
Like heroes they slaughtered the foe,
Till two hundred Indians or more, as they say,
Were slain by the Ohio.

The army of Indians were routed, and fled,
Our heroes pursued the foe,
While eighty soldiers and Charley lay dead,
On the banks of the Ohio.

The Brave Colonel Field and the gallant Buford,
Captains Wilson and Murray also,
And Allen, McClennahan, Goldsby and Ward,
Were slain by the Ohio.

Col. Fleming, and Mathews, and Shelby and Moore,
And Elliot, and Dillon, also,
And soldiers one hundred and thirty and four
Were wounded by the Ohio.

Farewell, Colonel Lewis, till pity's sweet fountains
Are dried in the hearts of the fair and the brave,
Virginia shall weep for her Chief of the mountains
And mourn for the heroes who sleep by his grave.

As Israel mourned for Moses of old,
In the valley of Moab by Nebow
We'll mourn for Charles Lewis the hero so bold,
Who fell by the Ohio.

As Israel did mourn and her daughters did weep,
For Saul and his host at Gilboa
We'll mourn Colonel Field and the heroes who sleep
On the banks of the Ohio.

Harry Maxwell Smythe was a native of Virginia who abandoned
the profession of law for that of journalism. When about forty years
of age he came to Moundsville, West Virginia, about 1872, and with
George A. Creel, he established *The New State Gazette,* a publication which had but a brief existence. Later he removed to Kansas
City, Missouri, where he died in 1883. In August 1875, there was a
great flood in the Ohio river. Mr. Smythe was then at Point Pleasant where he wrote the following, which appeared in the *Moundsville
Reporter* at that time :—

BATTLE OF POINT PLEASANT—A CENTENNIAL ODE.

An hundred years have breathed their changeful breath
    Upon this field of glory and of death;
A century of change, yet round me still,
    The self-same valley, plain, and glen and hill.
Where all day long the sound of battle rolled;
    Where all day long the fearful and the bold
Behind their slender bulwarks, stern and pale,
    Stood face to face, the white man and the red,
Their cause the same, the same their gory bed.

The same great rivers meet and mingle here,
That on that day of doubt, and dread and fear,
    Flowed camly on, unheedful of the strife,
The sound of battle and the wreck of life.
    Now sweet the sunlight falls upon the dell,
Where heroes fought and brave Charles Lewis fell.

Today when rains have swollen the river's tide,
The rich soil crumbles from the water's side;
  There white and ghastly, bedded in the clay,
The bones of those who fell that Autumn day;
    And ere they sink beneath Ohio's wave,
The sunlight, for a while, gleams in the grave
  Of sires of noble sons, and sons of noble sires;
A nation's incense, all her alter fires,
  Can scarce repay the labor of that day,
From dewy dawn, till sunlight fled away.

A nation's songs, through all the coming time
Can scarce give language to thy thoughts sublime;
  As standing there beside the crimson'd rills
You thought of dear ones far across the hills,
  Of West Augusta homes, where warm and bright,
The firelight gleamed on household gods at night,
  And dawn awoke each weary, weary day,
When bright eyes waiting, watched the western way,
    For forms those eyes might never never greet;
For forms then stark in death, where two great rivers meet.

THE CORNSTALK MONUMENT AT POINT PLEASANT, WEST VIRGINIA.

Erected in memory of *Keigh-tugh-qua,* a chieftain of the Shawnee nation known to the Virginians as Cornstalk, his Indian name signifying a cornstalk, the chief support of his people; he commanded the Indian army at Point Pleasant, October 10, 1774; and was killed by the Whites at that place, November 10, 1777. It is four feet and three inches square at the base, and twelve feet high. Erected in the court-house yard, October 13, 1899, by Samuel H. Reynolds, who was in charge of the construction of Lock No. 11, in the Great Kanawha river; he contributed the stone and the inscription. Other expenses were borne by the citizens of the town. The monument was removed from near Sixth Street, to its present position August 7, 1909. Cornstalk's grave is South 45° East 118 feet from the base of the monument.

"Cornstalk died a grand death, by an act of cowardly treachery on the part of his American foes; it is one of the darkest stains on the checkered pages of frontier history."—Roosevelt's *Winning of the West,"* Vol: I., p. 24.

CHAPTER XII.

Many persons have an impression that Cornstalk, the famous Shawnee chieftain who led the savage forces at Point Pleasant, was killed in the battle at that place. This is not true. His tragic death occurred there November 10, 1777. We have seen that at the treaty of Camp Charlotte, Captain William Russell with his company was detailed to build a fort at Point Pleasant. This was done and the little stockade received the name of "Fort Blair." It was abandoned by Captain Russell in June 1775, by direction of Lord Dunmore, and a few days later, the deserted stockade was burned by the Indians. In the autumn of that year, Captain Mathew Arbuckle with a body of troops, arrived at Point Pleasant and erected another stockade which received the name of "Fort Randolph." Here Captain Arbuckle continued in command of the garrison for more than two years, and it was while he was here that Cornstalk, his son Ellinipisco, and Red Hawk, a chief of the Delaware nation, suffered death at the hands of enraged Virginians. It is fortunate for the truth of history, that Captain John Stuart, the historian of Lord Dunmore's War, was present and an eye-witness of the tragic scene. He has left to us the following graphic account of it.[1]

"In the year 1777, the Indians, being urged by British agents, became very troublesome to frontier settlements, manifesting much appearance of hostilities, when the Cornstalk warrior, with the Red-hawk, paid a visit to the garrison at Point Pleasant. He made no secret of the disposition of the Indians; declaring that, on his own part, he was opposed to joining in the war on the side of the British, but that all the nation except himself and his own tribe, were determined to engage in it; and that, of course, he and his tribe would have to run with the stream, (as he expressed it.) On this Captain Arbuckle thought proper to de-

---

1. See Stuart's "Memoirs of the Indian Wars and Other Occurrences," pp. 16-20.

tain him, the Red Hawk, and another fellow, as hostages, to prevent the nation from joining the British.

In the course of that summer our government had ordered an army to be raised, of volunteers, to serve under the command of General Edward Hand; who was to have collected a number of troops at Fort Pitt, with them to descend the river to Point Pleasant there to meet a re-enforcement of volunteers expected to be raised in Augusta and Botetourt counties, and then proceed to the Shawnee towns and chastize them so as to compel them to a neutrality. Hand did not succeed in the collection of troops at Fort Pitt; and but three or four companies were raised in Augusta and Botetourt, which were under the command of Colonel George Skillern, who ordered me to use my endeavors to raise all the volunteers I could get in Greenbrier, for that service. The people had begun to see the difficulties attendant on a state of war and long campaigns carried through wildernesses, and but few were willing to engage in such service. But as the settlements which we covered, though less exposed to the depredations of the Indians, had showed their willingness to aid in the proposed plan to chastize the Indians, and had raised three companies, I was very much desirous of doing all I could to promote the business and aid the service. I used the utmost endeavors and proposed to the militia officers to volunteer ourselves, which would be an encouragement to others, and by such means to raise all the men who could be got. The chief of the officers in Greenbrier agreed to the proposal, and we cast lots who should command the company. The lot fell on Andrew Hamilton for captain, and William Renick lieutenant. We collected in all, about forty, and joined Colonel Skillern's party (at old Camp Union) on their way to Point Pleasant.

When we arrived, there was no account of General Hand or his army, and little or no provision made to support our troops, other than what we had taken with us down the Kenawha. We found, too, that the garrison was unable to spare us any supplies, having nearly exhausted, when we got there, what had been provided for themselves. But we concluded to wait there as long as we could for the arrival of General Hand, or some account from him. During the time of our stay two young men, of the names of Hamilton and Gilmore, went over the Kenawha one day to hunt for deer; on their return to camp, some Indians had concealed themselves on the bank amongst the weeds, to view our encampment; and as Gilmore came along past them, they fired on him and killed him on the bank.

Captain Arbuckle and myself were standing on the opposite bank when the gun fired; and whilst we were wondering who it could be shooting, contrary to orders, or what they were doing over the river, we saw Hamilton run down the bank, who called out that Gilmore was killed.

Gilmore was one of the company of Captain John Hall, of that part of the country now Rockbridge county. The Captain was a relation of Gilmore's, whose family and friends were chiefly cut off by the Indians, in the year 1763, when Greenbrier was cut off. Hall's men instantly jumped into a canoe and went to the relief of Hamilton, who was standing in momentary expectation of being put to death. They brought the corpse of Gilmore down the bank, covered with blood and scalped, and put him into the canoe. As they were passing the river, I observed to Captain Arbuckle that the people would be for killing the hostages, as soon as the canoe would land. He supposed that they would not offer to commit so great a violence upon the innocent, who were in nowise accessary to the murder of Gilmore. But the canoe had scarcely touched the shore until the cry was raised, let us kill the Indians in the fort; and every man, with his gun in his hand, came up the bank pale with rage. Captain Hall, was at their head, and leader. Captain Arbuckle and I met them and endeavored to dissuade them from so unjustifiable an action; but they cocked their guns, threatened us with instant death if we did not desist, rushed by us into the fort, and put the Indians to death.

On the preceding day, the Cornstalk's son, Ellinipsico,[2] had come from the nation to see his father, and to know if he was well, or alive. When he came to the river opposite the fort, he halloowed. His father was, at that instant, in the act of delineating a map of the country and the waters between the Shawnee towns and the Mississippi, at our request, with chalk upon the floor. He immediately recognized the voice of his son, got up, went out, and answered him. The young fellow crossed over, and they embraced each other in the most tender and affectionate manner. The interpreter's wife, who had been a prisoner among the Indians, and had recently left them on hearing the uproar the next day, and hearing the men threatening that they would kill the Indians, for whom she retained much affection, ran to their cabin and informed them that the people were just coming to kill them; and that, because the Indians who killed Gilmore, had come with Ellinipsico the day before; He utterly denied it; declared that he knew nothing of them, and trembled exceedingly. His father encouraged him not to be afraid for that the Great Man above had sent him there to be killed and die with him. As the men advanced to the door, the Cornstalk rose up and met them; they fired upon him, and seven or eight bullets went through him. So fell the great Cornstalk warrior,—whose name was bestowed upon him by the consent of the nation, as their great strength and support. His son was shot dead, as he sat upon a stool. The Red-Hawk made an attempt to go up the chimney, but was shot down. The other Indian was

---

2. Doubtless an English corruption of Al-lan-i-wis-i-ca.

shamefully mangled, and I grieved to see him so long in the agonies of death.

The Cornstalk, from personal appearance and many brave acts, was undoubtedly a hero. Had he been spared to live, I believe he would have been friendly to the American cause; for nothing could induce him to make the visit to the garrison at the critical time he did, but to communicate to them the temper and disposition of the Indians, and their design of taking part with the British. On the day he was killed we held a council, at which he was present. His countenance was dejected; and he made a speech, all of which seemed to indicate an honest and manly disposition. He acknowledged that he expected that he and his party would have to run with the stream, for that all the Indians on the lakes and northwardly, were joining the British. He said that when he returned to the Shawnee towns after the battle at the Point, he called a council of the nation to consult what was to be done, and upbraided them for their folly in not suffering him to make peace on the evening before the battle—'What,' said he, 'will you do now? The Big Knife is coming on us and we shall all be killed. Now you must fight, or we are undone.' But no one made an answer. He said, then let us kill all our women and children, and go and fight till we die. But none would answer. At length he rose and struck his tomahawk in the post in the center of the town house; 'I'll go,' said he, 'and make peace;' and then the warriors grunted out 'ough, ough, ough,' and runners were instantly despatched to the Governor's army to solicit a peace and the interposition of the Governor on their behalf.

When he made his speech in council, with us, he seemed to be impressed with an awful premonition of his approaching fate; for he repeatedly said, 'When I was a young man and went to war, I thought that might be the last time, and I would return no more. Now I am here among you; you may kill me if you please; I can die but once; and it is all one to me, now or another time.' This declaration concluded every sentence of his speech. He was killed about one hour after our council.

A few days after this catastrophe General Hand arrived, but had no troops. We were discharged and returned home a short time before Christmas. Not long after we left the garrison a small party of Indians appeared near the fort, and Lieutenant Moore was ordered with a party to pursue them. Their desire was to retaliate the murder of Cornstalk. Moore had not pursued one-quarter of a mile until he fell into an ambuscade and was killed, with several of his men."

EFFORTS TO PUNISH THE MEN WHO KILLED CORNSTALK:—Captain Stuart states that the company of Captain James Hall was from "that part of the country now Rockbridge county, Virginia."

This county was formed by act of the Assembly in 1777, and the first Court held therefor, convened at the house of Samuel Wallace where Lexington now stands April 7, 1778, but five months after Cornstalk was killed. The following is taken from the records of that Court:—

"April 30, 1778.—At a court held this day in the second year of the Commonwealth for the examination of Captain James Hall, who stands bound in recognizance for his appearance, charged with suspicion of felony in being concerned in the murder of the Cornstalk Indian, his son Ellinipsico, Redhawk, and another chief of the Indians on the 10th day of November last, there were present Charles Campbell, Samuel Lyle, Alexander Stewart and John Trimble, gentlemen. The above named James Hall appeared, and upon examination desired the facts with which he was charged, whereupon the sheriff proclaimed who could give evidence against the prisoner in behalf of the Commonwealth to appear and do the same, but none appeared. The Court were of the opinion that the said James Hall be further bound to appear before a court to be held for his examination on the 28th day of this instant, which he agreed to and entered into recognizance accordingly." At the appointed time he again appeared, was placed on trial and acquitted. Similar entries appear showing that Hugh Galbraith, Malcolm McCown and William Rowan were each tried upon the same charge and acquitted.[3]

Captains Arbuckle and Stuart gave respectful burial to Cornstalk and those who perished with him, the graves being located at what was afterward the corner of Viand and Kanawha Streets in the town of Point Pleasant, where they were kept marked. Stephen T. Mitchell, Editor of *The Spirit of the Old Dominion,* published at Richmond, Virginia, was at Point Pleasant in 1827. The inhabitants pointed out the grave of Cornstalk and he wrote the following:

"The remains of the warriors—Cornstalk and his son Ellinipsico—lie alone beneath the sod of the common as if their bodies, even in death disdained to have communication with those of the treacherous foe by whom they were slaughtered, whilst depending on their pledges of faith and hospitality. A slight mound of earth scarcely distinguished from the plain around it marks the tomb of the most relentless, yet the most generous foe that ever menaced the frontiers of America."[4]

In 1840, when the streets mentioned above were opened, the bones of these warriors were removed with military honors, and re-interred

---

3. See first Order-Book in Clerk's office of Rockbridge county, Virginia.
4. *Spirit of the Old Dominion,* No. 3, Vol. I., p. 155.

all together in one common grave, in the Court-House yard, at a
spot where a westward extension of the north wall of the old jail,
bisects a southern extension of the east wall of the Court-House,
about twenty-five feet from the southeast corner thereof.   Prior to
the Civil war, Mr Charles Rawson, a son of the jailor of the county,
at his own expense, put a rail fence around the grave, and his sister, Miss Susan, in the kindness of her heart, planted rose-bushes on
and about it; but during the occupation of the town by the armies,
in the Civil War, the rails were burned, and stock destroyed the
shrubbery.   Since then, it has been a neglected spot, but now—in
1909—it has been enclosed with concrete columns and connecting
chains, and otherwise beautified.   This work has been done by the
principal—Miss Bertha J. Steinbach—and students of the Point
Pleasant High School.

ADDENDA.

CORNSTALK was a name that once thrilled the heart of every
man on the Virginia frontier and struck terror into every inmate
of a mountain home.   He had no youth in history; the first known
of him being his connection with the Muddy creek massacre in
1763, in Greenbrier, and that of Carr's creek now in Rockbridge
county, a little later.   He was gifted with oratory, statesmanship,
heroism, a military strategist, straight in form, and majestic in movement.   It was his anxiety to preserve the frontier of Virginia from
desolation and death that prompted him to make his visit to Point
Pleasant, and the untimely and perfidious manner of his death caused
a deep and lasting regret to prevade the bosoms even of those who were
enemies of his nation.

Colonel Benjamin Wilson, afterward prominent in the affairs of
Monongalia, Harrison and Randolph counties, West Virginia, was
with Dunmore at Camp Charlotte and heard the speech of Cornstalk.   Of it he said:—

"When he arose, he was in no wise confused or daunted, but spoke
in a distinct voice, without stammering or repetition, and with peculiar
emphasis.   His looks, while addressing Dunmore, were truly grand and

majestic; yet graceful and attractive. I have heard the first orators in Virginia—Patrick Henry and Richard Henry Lee—but never have I heard one whose powers of delivery surpassed those of Cornstalk."[5]

RED-HAWK was a chieftain of the Delaware nation and like Ellinipisco, had been in the thickest of the fight at the battle of Point Pleasant. He was the chief speaker in behalf of the Indians at the treaty with Colonel Boquet at the Forks of Muskingum, November 12, 1764, where he said:—

"Brother, listen to us your younger brothers. As we see something in your eyes that looks dissatisfaction, we now clear them. You have credited bad stories against us. We clean your ears, that you may hear better hereafter. We wish to remove everything bad from your heart, that you may be as good as your ancesters. (A belt) We saw you coming with an uplifted tomahawk in your hand. We now take it from you, and throw it up to God. Let him do with it as he pleases. We hope never to see it more. Brother, as you are a warrior, take hold of this chain (handing a belt) of friendship, and let us think no more of war, in pity of our old men, women and children. We, too, are warriors."[6]

The remarkable figure made use of in this speech, of throwing the hatchet up to God, is new; and it was remarked by Thomas Hutchins, afterward the first Geographer of the United States, who heard it, that by it the speaker wished probably to be understood that, by this disposition of it, it would be out of the reach of bad men, and would be given only to the party in the future, to whom the right of revenge belonged; whereas if it were buried in the ground, any miscreant might dig it up * * * Red-Hawk promised, on behalf of his nation, that all the prisoners should be delievered up at Fort Pitt the next spring.

ELLINIPSICO though having at first appeared disturbed, met his death with great composure. He was shot upon the seat on which he was sitting. He had been beside his father throughout the battle day at Point Pleasant in 1774. Cornstalk had a son, THE WOLF, who was one of the Shawnee hostages taken by Dunmore to Williamsburg, and after escaping, was connected with some of the events on the border in the early years of the Revolution.

---

5. Drake's "Indians of North America." Book V., p. 546.
6. Drake's "Indians of North America," Book V., p. 695.

APPENDIX A.

THE ONLY ROSTERS PRESERVED OF THE COMPANIES WHICH WERE IN
THE BATTLE OF POINT PLEASANT, OR ARRIVED WITH COLONEL
CHRISTIAN IN THE EVENING AFTER IT HAD BEEN
FOUGHT AND WON.

But few of the rolls of Companies which participated in the battle
of Point Pleasant, or which arrived on the field that evening with
Colonel William Christian, are known to be in existence. Far the
greater number have been lost in the shades of oblivion. It is possible that some others, in addition to those we now have, may yet be
found, among the musty and dusty documents of public record offices
and libraries; but this is not probable. There were eleven companies in the Augusta Regiment, under Colonel Charles Lewis; eight
companies in the Botetourt Regiment, under Colonel William Fleming; and seven companies in the Fincastle Battalion, under Colonel
William Christian. In addition thereto, there were one company
of Minute Men from Culpeper county, under Colonel John Field,
(acting Captain); a company of Volunteers from Dunmore (now
Shenandoah) county, commanded by Captain Thomas Slaughter;
a company of Riflemen from Bedford county, at the head of which
was Captain Thomas Buford; and a company of Kentucky Pioneers, led on by Captain James Harrod. Of the rolls of these companies—thirty in number—only the following eleven are known to
exist. We print them by permission of the copyright proprietors,
from Thwaites and Kellogg's "Documentary History of Dunmore's
War;" the originals being in the library of the State Historical
Society of Wisconsin.

IN THE AUGUSTA COUNTY REGIMENT.

A LIST OF CAPTAIN WILLIAM NALLE'S COMPANY OF VOLUNTEERS IN THE
AUGUSTA COUNTY REGIMENT.

OFFICERS.

William Nalle, ...Captain,

Martin Nalle, ...Lieutenant,
Jacob Pence, ...Ensign,
John Bush, ...Sergeant,
William Bush, ...Sergeant,
Bernard Crawford, ...Sergeant.

PRIVATES.

Shadrick Butler,	John Owler,
William Feavill,	George Fuls (or Fultz,)
Robert Hains,	James Miller,
Moses Smith,	George Harmon,
Stephen Washburn,	John Chisholm,
Israel Meaders,	Adam Hansbarger,
Henry Owler,	Henry Cook,
John Griggsby,	John Breden,
Richard Welch,	Thomas Brooke,
Zacarias Lee,	Henry Miner,
John Goodall,	Chesley Rogers,
Benjamin Petty,	Zapaniah Lee,
Michael Jordan,	Zachlaus Plunkenpiel,
Bruten Smith,	Micajah Smith,
James Todd,	William Smith,
William Spicer,	John Deck,
James Washburn,	John Fry,
Charles Brown,	John Williams,
James Alexander,	Joseph Butler,
George Rucker,	James Selby,
Joseph Ray (or Roay),	James Reary,
William Scales,	Abraham Rue,
John Bright,	Jacob Null,
Yenty Jackson,	John Null.

Total 54.

IN THE BOTETOURT COUNTY REGIMENT.

A List of Captain John Murray's Company of Volunteers in the Botetourt County Regiment.

OFFICERS.

John Murray ....Captain,*
William McKee ....Lieutenant,**
Samuel Wallace ....Lieutenant,
Adam Wallace ....Ensign,
William Taylor ....Sergeant,

---

*Killed at Point Pleasant.
**Assumed command of the company when Captain Murray was killed.

Moses Coiler ....Sergeant,
John Larken ....Sergeant,
John Simpson ....Sergeant,
Barney Boyls ....Sergeant,

PRIVATES.

John Gilmore,
Hugh Logan,
James Hall,
James Arnold,
Stephen Arnold,
William Moore,
John Nelson,
John Sedbury,
William MacCorkle,
George Milwood,
Andrew Evans,
Joseph McBride,
Thomas Nail,
John Lapsly,
James Walker,
Ezekiel Kennedy,
John Jones,
John Moore,
William Simpson,
Thomas McClure,
Peter Cassady,
Robert Wallace,
Thomas Pearry,
John Griggs,
George Cummings,
John Eager (or Edgar),
James Crawley,
Daniel Blair,
Thomas Burney,
Daniel Simpkins,
William Lyons,
James Simpkins,
Nicholas Mooney,
Solomon Brundige,

John McClure,
Stephen Harris,
Daniel Fullin (or Pullin),
David Wallace,
Moses Whitby,
James Gilmore,
James Cunningham,
John Kelsey,
Hugh Moore,
Joseph Gibson,
William Cochran,
James Logan,
John Logan,
Thomas Hedden,
Prisley Gill,
John Coiler,
Jonathan Watson,
Hugh Logan,
William Neely,
James Neely,
John Miligan,
Peter Higgings,
William Conner,
William Bradley,
John McGee,
William Brown,
James McCalister,
John Barkley,
Andrew Wallace,
Isaac Trimble,
Peter McNeal,
William Johns,
Andrew Alden,
James Brambridge,
John Murray.   —Total 78.

A LIST OF CAPTAIN PHILIP LOVE'S COMPANY OF VOLUNTEERS, IN THE BOTETOURT COUNTY REGIMENT.

OFFICERS.

Philip Love ....Captain,
Daniel McNeill ....Lieutenant,
John Mills ....Ensign,
William Ewing ....Sergeant Major,
Francis McElhaney ....Quarter M. S.,
Shelton Taylor.........................Sergeant,
James Alexander* ....Sergeant,
John Crawford ....Sergeant,

PRIVATES.

Robert Owen,	James Neeley,
Samuel Andrews,	Abraham Moon,
William Scott,	George Craig,
Samuel MtGumery (Montgomery)	Richard Wilson,
William Teasy,	Robert Smith,
John Todd,	John Buchanan,
Thomas Pierce,	Charles Davis,
Thomas Armstrong,	William Franklin,
John Dunn,	James Franklin,
Charles Byrne,	William Hanson,
Thomas Gilbert,	James McDonald,
Abraham DeMonts,	Richard Collins,
William Hooper,	James M. Guillin,
Samuel Savage,	John McGinnis,
Thomas Welch,	Griffin Harriss,
Thomas Welch, Jr.	John Jones,
Patrick Conner,	John Marks,
Joseph Pain,	John Robinson,
William Armstrong,	John Todd,
Daniel McDonald,	Daniel Ormsbey.
James Simpson,	—Total 50.
Thomas Brown,	

A LIST OF CAPTAIN JOHN LEWIS'* COMPANY OF VOLUNTEERS IN THE BOTETOURT COUNTY REGIMENT.

OFFICERS.

John Lewis ....Captain,

*Wounded at Point Pleasant.
*This Captain John Lewis was a son of General Andrew Lewis, and a cousin of Captain John Lewis, (son of Thomas) of the Augusta Regiment, his father being a brother of the General.—V. A. L.

John Henderson ....Lieutenant,
Robert Alliet (Eliott) ....Ensign,
Samuel Glass, ...Sergeant,
William Bryans ....Sergeant,
Peter Huff ....Sergeant,
William Wilson ....Sergeant,
Samuel Estill ....Sergeant,
John Donnally ....Fifer,
Thomas Alsbury ....Drummer,

PRIVATES.

John Swope,
Alexander Kelley,
Edward Eagin,
James Ellison,
John Deniston,
James Stuart,
John Savage,
Christopher Welch,
James Crawley,
James Dulin,
Isaac Fisher,
Peter Ellenburg,
Andrew Kissinger,
Samuel Barton,
William Clifton,
Joseph Love,
Leonard Huff,**
Thomas Huff,**
Samuel Croley,
William Isum,
Isaac Taylor,
Martin Carney,
Peter Hendricks,
John Hundley,
Henry Howard,
Molastine Peregrine,
Walter Holwell,
James McNutt,
Samuel Burcks,
Nathan Farmer,
Gabriel Smithers,

Thomas Edgar,
James Carlton,
Matthew Polug (or Pogue),
Thomas Canady (or Kanady),
William Jones,
Richard Packwood,
John Arthur,
William Robinson,
Samuel Huff,
Edward Wilson,
Robert Boyd,
John Reyburn,
Isaac Nichol,
Philip Hammond,
James Burtchfield,
Solomon White,
Thomas Carpenter,**
Jeremiah Carpenter,
Solomon Carpenter,
David Cook,
John Bowman,
Jacob Bowman,
Robert Bowles,
James Burnsides,
Dennis Nail,
Hugh Caperton,
Matthew Creed,
Matthew Jewitt,
Adam Cornwell,
William Boniface,
Robert Davis,

**Wounded at Point Pleasant.

John Carpenter,   Henry Bowyer,
Thomas Burnes,   Mathias Kissinger,
Adam Caperton,   William Mann.

—Total 78.

A LIST OF CAPTAIN JOHN STEWART'S COMPANY OF GREENBRIER VALLEY
    VOLUNTEERS IN THE BOTETOURT COUNTY REGIMENT.

OFFICERS.

John Stuart ....Captain,
(Manuscript torn) ....
James Donnally ....Sergeant,
Charles O'Hara...........................Sergeant,
Skidmore Harriman ....Sergeant,

PRIVATES.

Daniel Workman,   William Dyer,
Samuel Williams,   Edward Smith,
William O'Harra,   John Harris,
Robert O'Harra,   Joseph Currence,
James Pauley,   William Clendenin,
James Clarke,   Spencer Cooper,
John Pauley,   Daniel Taylor,
Archibald McDowell,   Joseph Day,
William Hogan,   Jacob Lockhart,
Andrew Gardiner,   George Clendennin,
Quavy Lockhart,   John Burke,
Samuel Sullivan,   Charles Kennison,*
Thomas Ferguson,*   William Ewing,
John McCandless   John Doherty,
Thomas Gillispie,   John McNeal,
Henry Lawrence,   Joseph Campbell,   —Total 37.
John Crain,

A LIST OF CAPTAIN ROBERT MCCLENNAHAN'S COMPANY OF GREENBRIER
    VALLEY VOLUNTEERS IN THE BOTETOURT COUNTY REGIMENT.

OFFICERS.

Robert McClennahan ....Captain,
William McCoy ....Lieutenant,
Mathew Bracken, ...Ensign,*
Thomas Williams ....Sergeant,

*Wounded at Point Pleasant.
*Killed at Point Pleasant.

William Craig .... Sergeant,
Samuel Clarke .... Sergeant,
William Jones .... Drummer,

PRIVATES.

John Harmon,
James Kinkaid,
George Kinkaid,
David Cutlip,
James Morrow, Sr.,
James Morrow, Jr.,
James Gilkeson,
Evan Evans,
William Stewart,
Edward Thomas,
Patrick Constantine,
William Custer,
Lewis Holmes,
William Hutchinson,

Edward Barrett,
John Williams,
Richard Williams,
James Burrens,
John Patton,
Thomas Ellias,
Charles Howard,
James Guffy,
Thomas Cooper
William McCaslin,
John Cunningham,
Francis Boggs,
John Vaughn.   —Total 34.

A LIST OF CAPTAIN HENRY PAULING'S COMPANY OF VOLUNTEERS OF THE BOTETOURT COUNTY REGIMENT.

OFFICERS.

Henry Pauling .... Captain,
Edward Goldman .... Lieutenant,*
Samuel Baker .... Ensign,
Obediah H. Trent .... Sergeant
Robert Findley .... Sergeant
James Woods, ... Sergeant.

PRIVATES.

Robert Watkins
Philip Hanes,
James DeHority,
William Thompson,
William Holley,
Joel Doss,
William Ray,
Dangerfield Harmon,
Stephen Holston,
James Wilson,
Dudley Callaway,

William Canaday,
John Clerk,
John Frazer,
George Davis,
Thomas McCrary,
Richard Rollins,
Michael Looney,
John Gibson,
Charles Ellisson,
John Agnew,
James Donahoo,

*Wounded in Battle of Point Pleasant.

David Belew,
Andrew Rogers,
Robert Ferrell,
Andrew Harrison,
George Zimmerman,
Thomas Wilson,
Alexander Caldwell,
William Gilliss,
Edward Ross,
Matthew Ratcliff,
William Glass,
John Fitzhugh,

Thomas Reid,
Joseph Whittaker,
Isham Fienquay,
David Condon,
Richard LeMaster,
James King,
John Hutson,
William McCalister,
Jeremiah Jenkins,
Edward Carther,
Martin Baker,
James Lynn,　　　　—Total 52.

THE FINCASTLE COUNTY BATTALION.

A LIST OF CAPTAIN EVAN SHELBY'S COMPANY OF VOLUNTEERS FROM THE WATAUGA VALLEY, IN THE FINCASTLE COUNTY BATTALION.

OFFICERS.

Evan Shelby ....Captain,*
Isaac Shelby ....Lieutenant,**
James Robertson ....Sergeant,
Valentine Levier ....Sergeant,

PRIVATES.

James Shelby,
John Sawyer,
John Findley,
Henry Shaw, (Span)
Daniel Mungle (Mongle),
Frederick Mungle,
John Williams,
John Carmack,†
Andrew Terrence, (Torrence),
George Brooks,
Isaac Newland,
Abram Newland,
George Ruddle (Riddle),
Emanuel Shoatt,
Abram Bogard,

Arthur Blackburn,
Robert Herrill (Handley),
George Armstrong,
William Casey,
Mark Williams,
John Stewart,†
Conrad Nave,
Richard Burck,
John Riley,
Elijah Robison, (Robertson),
Reece Price,†
Richard Holliway,
Jarrett Williams,
Julias Robison,
Charles Fielder,

*Assumed chief command on the field of battle after Colonels Lewis, Fleming, and Field had fallen.
**Took command of his father's company, who had assumed command on the field.
†Wounded at Point Pleasant.

Peter Torney (Forney,)
William Tucker,
Jonn Fain,
Samuel Vance,
Samuel Fain ,
Samuel Hensley, (Handley),
Samuel Samples,

Benjamin Grayum (Graham)
Andrew Goff,
Hugh O'Gullion,
Barnett O'Gullion,
Patrick St. Lawrence,
Joseph Hughey (James Hughey)
John Bradley,
Bazaleel Maxwell.   —Total 49.

A Partial List of Captain William Campbell's Company* in the Fincastle County Battalion.

OFFICERS.

William Campbell ....Captain,

PRIVATES.

Philemon Hoggins,
Benjamin Richardson,
Joseph Newberry,
John Johnston,
Stephen Hopton,
Richard Woolsey,
John Lewis,
Auldin Williamson,

William Hopton,
Coonrad Sterns,
John Neil,
Wiliam Richardson,
Richard Lyhnam,
William Champ,
John Boles.   —Total 15.

A List of Captain James Harrod's Company of Kentucky Pioneers in the Fincastle County Battalion.

(From Collin's "History of Kentucky," Vol II, p. 517.)

OFFICERS.

James Harrod ....Captain,*

PRIVATES.

James Blair,
James Brown,
Abraham Chapline,

James Harlan,
James Harrod,
Thomas Harrod,

---

* There were 39 men in Captain Campbell's Company, but the names of only 15 of them have been preserved.

*In the spring of 1774, Captain James Harrod, a Pennsylvanian by birth, collected at the mouth of Grave Creek, now Moundsville, Marshall county, West Virginia, a party of thirty-one young men, for the purpose of making a settlement in Kentucky. Descending the Ohio to the mouth of the Kentucky river, they thence journeyed through the wilderness to the Big Spring, now in Mercer county. Here they were engaged in founding Harrodsburg, the oldest town in Kentucky, when they were discovered by Daniel Boone and Michael Stoner who had been sent by Lord Dunmore to warn John Floyd, Deputy Surveyor of Fincastle county, Virginia, which then included all of Kentucky, together with his assistants, then at the Falls of the Ohio, that an Indian War was begun. Harrod and party abandoned their settlement, and proceeded to the Holston Valley, where he and twenty-seven of his men joined the Fincastle Battalion, and with Christian, arrived at Point Pleasant the evening after the battle.

John Clark,
John Crawford,
Jared Cowan,
John Cowan,
John Crow,
Azariah Davis,
William Fields,
Robert Gilbert,
David Glenn,
Thomas Glenn,
James Hamilton,
Silas Harlan,

Evan Hinton,
Isaac Hite,
James Knox,
James McCulloch,
Alexander Petrey,
Azariah Reece,
Jacob Sandusky,
John Shelp,
James Sodousky,
Benjamin Tutt,
James Wiley,
David Williams,
John Wilson.   —Total 32.

THE INDEPENDENT COMPANIES.

Of the Independent Companies,—the Dunmore County Volunteers, the Culpepper Minute Men, and the Bedford County Riflemen,—but one roster, that of the latter, has been preserved. This follows:—

A LIST OF CAPTAIN THOMAS BUFORD'S COMPANY OF BEDFORD COUNTY RIFLE COMPANY OF VOLUNTEERS.

OFFICERS.

Thomas Buford ....Captain,*
Thomas Dooley ....Lieutenant,
Jonathan Cundiff ....Ensign,
Nicholas Mead ....Sergeant,
William Kenedy ....Sergeant,
John Fields, ...Sergeant,
Thomas Fliping ....Sergeant.

PRIVATES.

Abraham Sharp,
Absalom McClanahan,
William Bryant,
William McColister,
James Scarbara,
John McClanahan,
James McBride,
John Carter,
Adam Lynn,
Thomas Stephens,

Thomas Hall,
William Hamrick,
Nathaniel Cooper,
John Cook,
Mr. Waugh,
John McGlahlen,
John Campbell,
William Campbell,
Robert Boyd,
Thomas Hamrick,

*Died of wounds the night after the battle.

William Kerr,
Gerrott Kelley,
James Ard,
William Deal,
John Bozel,
John Welch,
William Overstreet,
Robert Hill,
Samuel Davis,
Zachariah Kennot,
Augustine Hackworth,
William Cook,
Uriah Squires,

James Boyd,
James Dale,
Robert Ewing,
Francis Seed,
William Hackworth,
John Roberts,
Joseph White,
Joseph Bunch,
Jacob Dooley,
Thomas Owen,
John Read,
John Wood,   —Total 52.

From the foregoing official rosters it will be seen that they contain five hundred and thirty-one names. If to these we add those of the captains, of the nineteen companies, whose names are known, but of which we have no rosters, we shall have a total of five hundred and fifty names of the men who were with the Southern Division, or left wing of Dunmore's Army, commanded by General Lewis.

Note—The "Documentary History of Dunmore's War" is the chief and by far the most reliable source from which to obtain rosters of the companies engaged in the battle of Point Pleasant, and we print therefrom all of those which participated in that struggle. In addition to these, that work contains rolls or lists of men engaged in defending the frontier in 1774. These included the companies of Captains Daniel Smith, page 396; Robert Doak, p. 399; men in Michael Woods' Muster District, p. 396; Thomas Burk's Muster District, p. 398; and the Garrisons at Elk Garden Fort, p. 401; at Glade Hollow Fort, p. 402; at Maiden Spring Station, and Upper Station, p. 403; and a list of scouts on p. 404. Not one of these organizations was in the battle of Point Pleasant, as is shown by the regimental and battalion organizations on pages 413, 414, 415, 416, 417, 418, of the said work.

APPENDIX B.

THE AFTER-LIFE OF THE MEN WHO FOUGHT THE BATTLE OF POINT
PLEASANT.

"It is worth noting that all the after time leaders of the West were engaged in some way in Lord Dunmore's War."—Roosevelt's *"Winning of the West."* Vol. I, p. 242.

"This battle was the most bloody and the best contested in the annals of forest warfare. The heroes of that day proved themselves worthy to found States."— Bancroft's *"History of the United States."* Vol. IV, p.87.

How true are these statements of eminent historians! They won the battle of Point Pleasant, which changed the course of history on this continent; and when the War for Independence came, they met the heroes of Lexington, Concord, and Bunker Hill, and together with them, were at Monmouth, Brandywine, King's Mountain, and York-town. Seven officers in the Battle of Point Pleasant rose to the rank of general in the Revolutionary Army; six captains in that battle commanded regiments on continental establishment in the war for independence; four officers in that battle led the attack on Gwynn's Island, in Chesapeake Bay, in July 1776, which resulted in the dis-lodgement of Lord Dunmore, the late governor, who was thus driven from the shores of Virginia never to return; one captain in that battle was the most prominent American officer in the battle of Brandywine where he was severely wounded; another officer in that battle led the advance at the storming of Stony Point, one of the most daring achievements of the Revolution; still another officer in that battle, won lasting fame as the "Hero of King's Mountain." Hundreds of men in that battle were afterward on revolutionary fields and many of them witnessed the surrender of Cornwallis to the united armies of the United States and France, at the close of that struggle, at Yorktown. Indeed, it is a matter of history that these Point Pleasant men were on nearly every battlefield of the Revolution. And one of them, when sixty-three years of age, led the Americans at the battle of the Thames, in 1813, secured a great victory, and thus broke the English power in the Northwest.

But it was not alone on fields of carnage that the men who fought the battle of Point Pleasant, distinguished themselves. Six of them

afterwards occupied seats in the American House of Representatives;
three of them were members of the United States Senate; four of
them became governors of states; one of them a Lieutenant Governor; one of them a Territorial Governor; one of them military
and civil commandant of Upper Louisiana; one of them a surveyor-
general of one of the thirteen original states; one the father of a
governor of Virginia; one, the father of a supreme judge of Kentucky;
one of them the largest manufacturer and wealthiest man in eastern
Ohio at the time of his business career; one of them president of
the Bank of St. Louis; one of them a framer of a constitution for
Ohio; one of them a receiver of public monies in a western State;
and a hundred of them state legislators and framers of state con-
situations; while more than a thousand of them went forth to conquer
again—not with a rifle, but with the axe— that they might fell the
forests from which they had driven barbarism and change the land
into fruitful fields.

Was another such battle ever fought, by an army composed of
such men? Their fame then resounded, not only in the backwoods,
but throughout Virginia. Now, it is known to a nation. Historians
have not done them justice. Still, they have not been forgotten.
Their names are all around us. Of the men who made national
history at Point Pleasant, the name of one is preserved in that of a
county in Pennsylvania; the names of three in those of counties in
Ohio; of four of them in county names in Indiana; of four of them
in the names of counties in Illinois; of four of them in county
names in West Virginia; of five of them in the names of counties in
Tennessee; and ten of them in the names of counties in Kentucky.
Towns named in memory of men who were in the battle of Point
Pleasant are found in many states, prominent among them being
Christiansburg, Virginia; Lewisburg, and Clendenin, West Virginia;
Flemingsburg and Harrodsburg, Kentucky; Clarksville and Sevier-
ville, Tennessee; and Shelbyville, Indiana.

It was in commemoration of the historic achievement of these men
that a Nation and a State—the United States and West Virginia—
have united in rearing a towering and enduring monument on the
battlefield of Point Pleasant.

APPENDIX C.

The *Virginia Gazette,* the first newspaper published in that Colony, was founded at Williamsburg in 1736; and was the official Journal of the Colony, it was published in 1772 by William Rind; he died the next year and his wife, Clementina, assumed the management of the paper. She died September 24, 1774, after which it was continued for her children by her relative, John Pinkney, a prominent printer of that time. It was then the only newspaper published in the Colony. The following extracts relating to Dunmore's War are copied from it:

"It is reported, and we believe with too much certainty that an Indian War is inevitable, as many outrages have lately happened on the frontiers; but whether the Indians or White people are most to blame, we can not determine, the accounts being so extremely complicated."—*Virginia Gazette,* Thursday, May 26, 1774.

"We likewise hear that the Frontier inhabitants are all in motion at the behavior of the Indians, and seem determined to drive from among them so cruel and treacherous an enemy."—*Virginia Gazette,* Thursday, June 2, 1774.

Cave Cumberland writes the Gazette under date of June 21, 1774, saying:

"I have had no accounts of my brother since he left Fort Pitt, nor is there any news or word of any of the traders at the Shawnee towns. What has become of them, God only knows. But all accounts of that quarter are very bad. We have received accounts this day by express that one Captain McClure, a Virginian, is killed and another man mortally wounded, by a party of Indians which was out near Red Stone. All the poor people who were settled over the Allegheny mountains, are either moved off or gathered in large numbers and making places of defence to secure themselves."—*Virginia Gazette,* Thursday, July 14, 1774.

"Last Sunday morning his Excellency, our Governor, left this city in order to take a view of the situation of the frontier of this Colony. It seems his Lordship intends to settle matters amicably with the Indians if possible, and proposes to have conferences with the different Nations, to find out the causes of the late Disturbances."—*Virginia Gazette*, Thursday, July 14, 1774.

"Lord Dunmore before leaving Williamsburg, July 10th, issued a proclamation stating that the House of Burgesses was summoned to meet on Thursday, August 11, ensuing. He, because of absence on the Frontier, prorogued that body until the first Thursday in November next."—*Virginia Gazette*, Thursday, July 14, 1774.

"Wednesday evening last an express arrived in this city who reports that many families have very lately been barbously murdered on the Frontiers of Pennsylvania and Virginia, and that his Excellency, Lord Dunmore, is endeavoring all in his power to repel those hostile and inhuman savages. Colonel Preston and General Lewis, it seems, have raised a thousand men each, and it is reported also that a like number has enlisted under his Lordship's banner, he, as well as them, being greatly exasperated at the late cruel and intolerable treatment of the Indians towards the white people residing at or near the back parts of this Colony."—*Virginia Gazette*, Thursday, August 25, 1774.

"The Indians are daily committing some foul murder or other. Their cruel and inhuman treatment towards the people on the Frontiers loudly calls for vengeance."—*Virginia Gazette*, Thursday, September 8, 1774.

"His Excellency, Lord Dunmore, we hear has amicably settled matters with the Delaware, Wyandot, and Seneca Indians, who have lately brought many tokens of their peaceable disposition and of their determination to maintain peace. His Lordship, set off some time since with a detachment in order to compromise affairs with the other Nations and it is supposed that he will be equally successful."—*Virginia Gazette*, Thursday, October 6, 1774.

An extract of a letter from Colonel William Preston, dated Fincastle, September 28, 1774, states:—

"That part of the army under the command of General Lewis who is to meet Lord Dunmore at the mouth of the Great Kanawha, or New River, assembled at the 'Great Levels' of Greenbrier, to the amount of about fifteen hundred men, rank and file. Colonel Charles Lewis marched with about six hundred men on the 6th, for the mouth of Elk, a branch of New River which empties in some distance below the Falls, there to build a small fort, and to prepare canoes. General Andrew Lewis marched with another large party on the 12th instant for the same place, and Colonel Christian was to march yesterday (September 27th) with the remainder, being about four hundred, and the last supply of provisions. This body of Militia being mostly armed with Rifle Guns, and a great part of them good woodsmen, are looked upon to be at least equal to any Troops, for the number that have ever been raised in America. It is earnestly hoped that they will, in conjunction with the other party, be able to chastise the Ohio Indians for the many murders and robberies, they have committed on our Frontiers for many years past.

On the 8th instant, one John Harvey, was dangerously wounded and his wife and three children taken prisoners on the head of Clinch river. The man at that time made his escape, but is since dead of his wounds. The same day a man was taken prisoner by another party of the enemy, on the north Fork of the Holston. On the 13th a soldier was fired upon by the Indians on Clinch River; but as he received no hurt, he returned the fire and it is believed killed an Indian, as much blood was found where he fell and one of the plugs which burst out of his wound was also found. The soldier was supported by some men who were near, and gave the two Indians a chase; who it is supposed threw the wounded one into a deep Pit that was near. These parties of the enemy were pursued several days by Captain Daniel Smith; who could not overtake them, they having stolen horses to carry them off.

On the 23rd, two Negroes were taken prisoners at Blackmore's Fort, on Clinch River, and a great many horses and cattle shot down. On the 24th of September, a family was killed and taken at Reedy Creek, a branch of Holston, near the Cherokee Line; and on Saturday morning, the 25th, Hallooing, and the report of many guns, were heard at several houses, but the damage done was not known when the express came away. These last murders are believed to be perpetrated by the Cherokees, as two men lately returned from that country and made oath that two parties had left the towns, either to join the Shawnees, or to fall upon some of the Settlements; and that the Cherokees, in general, appeared in a very bad temper, which greatly alarmed the traders.

It is impossible to conceive the consternation into which the last stroke has put the inhabitants on Holston and Clinch rivers, and the latter as many of their choice men are on the expedition, and they have no ammunition. Two of these people were at my house this day, and, after traveling about a hundred miles, offered ten shillings a pound for powder; but there is none to be had for any money. Indeed, it is very alarming; for should the Cherokees engage in a war at this time it would ruin us, as so many men are out and ammunition is so scarce. Add to this the strength of those people, and their towns being so near our settlements on Holston."—*Virginia Gazette*, Thursday, October 13, 1774.

"This morning an express arrived in this city, from his Excellency, Lord Dunmore, with intelligence relative to his Lordship and the Indians. Far advanced as the week is, we think it our indispensible duty to com-

municate, at all times, anything that may be important to the public, and
have therefore given a supplement to this weeks paper."—*Virginia Gazette*, Thursday, October 14th, 1774.

THE FIRST PRINTED ACCOUNT OF THE BATTLE OF POINT PLEASANT:
—This appeared in the *Virginia Gazette* of November 10, 1774. Some
authorities say that it was written by Captain Mathew Arbuckle;
others that it was prepared by Lieutenant Isaac Shelby. The fact is
that is was written by Captain Thomas Slaughter, commanding the
Dunmore County Volunteers, on the battle-field, on the 17th of October, 1774. This he sent to his brother in Culpeper County, who
sent it to the *Gazette* for publication, it being accompanied by the
following letter:—

"Culpeper, (Va.), November 3, 1774.

Mr. Pinkney:—

I received yesterday, from my brother, by an express from the banks
of the Ohio, at the mouth of the Great Kanawha an account of a battle
between our troops and the Indians, which I have enclosed, to be inserted
in your Gazette, with a list of the killed and wounded. My brother, likewise, writes me of our Governor being still on his march to the Indian
towns, and as the account is certain, he may not be expected for some
time. His Excellency was not in the engagement, being about 75 miles
up the Ohio, on the Indian Side. An Express arrived from him the evening after the battle, with orders for their troops to meet him at some
distance from the towns so that when the express came off he had no account of the battle.

I am, Sir, your Obedient Servant,

FRANCIS T. SLAUGHTER."

Following this letter is a description of the battle which is substantially the same as that written by Lieutenant Isaac Shelby, and
printed elsewhere in this work.*

"In the afternoon of December 4, 1774, Lord Dunmore arrived at the
palace in this city from his expedition against the Indians who have been
humbled into a necessity of soliciting peace themselves and have delivered
hostages for the due observance of the terms which cannot fail of giving
satisfaction as thy confine the Indians to limits which entirely remove the
grounds of future quarrel between them and the people of Virginia and
lay a foundation for a fair and extensive Indian trade, which if properly
followed must produce the most beneficial effects to this country. We hear

---

*See ante. pp. 43, 44, 45.

that four of the principal Shawnee warriors are expected here in a few days, and that twelve head men and warriors of the Delaware and other nations are left at Fort Dunmore as hostages. The Indians have delivered up all the white prisoners in their towns, with the horses and other plunder they took from the inhabitants, and offered to give up their own horses. They have agreed to abandon the lands on this side of the Ohio, which river is to be the boundary between them and the white people and never more take up the hatchet against the English. Thus, in little more than the space of five months, an end is put to a war which portened much trouble and mischief to the inhabitants on the Frontier, owing to the zeal and good conduct of the officers and commanders who went out in their country's defense and the bravery and perservance of all the troops."—*Virginia Gazette*, Thursday, December 8, 1774.

APPENDIX D.

A PARTIAL LIST OF MEN WOUNDED IN THE BATTLE OF POINT PLEASANT,
WHO WERE AFTERWARD GRANTED PENSIONS BY THE
COMMONWEALTH OF VIRGINIA.

For the reason that the men who fought the battle of Point Pleasant were never included in any pension legislation of the United States, no pensions were ever paid by the General Government to any of the participants therein. It was a battle between Virginians and Indians, and for that reason, the Commonwealth of Virginia granted numerous pensions to her sons who were wounded in that conflict. Among these were the following:—

JOHN MCKENNEY, a member of Captain George Moffatt's Company; shot through the left thigh and wrist of the left arm, and cut by tomahawk between the shoulders; granted £20:00:0 for immediate use and £10:00:0 per annum during his life. (See "Journal of the House of Burgesses," session beginning June 1, 1775.)

ABRAM FIELD, one of the Culpeper County Minute Men in Colonel John Field's Company; wounded in right arm, unable to support wife and three small children; allowed the sum of £20:00:0 for present relief, and £10:00:0 per annum during his life. (See "Journal of the House of Burgesses," session beginning June 1, 1775.)

COLONEL WILLIAM FLEMING, commanding the Botetourt County Regiment; wounded in the breast and left arm, thus rendering him unable to practice his profession as a surgeon; granted £500:00:0 instead of a pension as a recompense for his gallant behavior and the wounds he received in this army. (See "Journal of the House of Burgesses," session beginning June 1, 1775.)

WILLIAM SHEPHERD, wounded in left shoulder and arm so that he was rendered unable to earn a subsistance; granted pension of £7:10:0 per annum during his life; also the sum of £16:14:2, to pay William Smith, a surgeon, for treating his wounds. (See "Journal of the House of Burgesses," session beginning June 1, 1775.)

WILLIAM LYNN, a Lieutenant wounded in action; granted £30:00:0 per annum during his life. (See "Journal of the House of Burgesses," session beginning June 1, 1775.)

ELIZABETH CROLEY, widow of Samuel Croley, killed in battle; granted £25:00:0 and the further sum of £10:00:0 per annum for ten years, to be disbursed by the Church-Wardens in the Parish of Camden, in the County of Pittsylvania, for her use during her widowhood or for her children by Samuel Croley, after the death or marriage of their mother. (See "Journal of the House of Burgesses," session beginning June 1, 1775.)

JOHN STEWART, wounded in the left arm, allowed the sum of £20:00:0 for his present relief. See Journal of the House of Delegates, session beginning October 20, 1777, p. 124.)

THOMAS PRICE, of Randolph County; granted pension of £15:00:0, December 16, 1790, payable annually. (See "Hening's Statutes at Large," Vol. XIII., p. 205.)

ALEXANDER STUART, in Captain Moffatt's Company; shot through the thighs; granted pension of £8:00:00 payable annually, December 20, 1792. (See "Hening's Statutes at large," Vol. XIII., p. 616.)

BENJAMIN BLACKBOURNE, Sergeant in Lewis' Augusta Regiment; granted pension of £15:00:0, payable annually, December 2, 1793. (See "Shepherd's Statutes at Large," Vol. I., p. 278. also "Hening's Statutes at Large," Vol. XIII., p. 616.)

JAMES ROBINSON, of Bath County; shot through the head; granted pension of £10:00:0, payable annually, December 22, 1794. (See "Shepherd's Statutes at Large," Vol. I., p. 332.)

JAMES CURRY, in Captain Moffatt's Company; shot through right elbow; granted pension of £5:00:0, payable annually, in 1776; died July 14, 1834. (See "Session Acts, General Assembly of Virginia," 1815-16, p. 256.)

APPENDIX E.

Nothing connected with General Lewis' army is more remarkable than the kinship existing among the men composing it. General Andrew Lewis and Colonel Charles Lewis, the latter killed in action, were brothers; Captain John Lewis (son of Andrew) commanding a company in the Botetourt Regiment, was of course a nephew of Colonel Charles Lewis; and Captain John Lewis, of the Augusta Regiment, son of Thomas (a brother of Andrew and Charles) was a nephew of both of them, and a cousin of Captain John Lewis of the Botetourt Regiment. Colonel Charles Lewis had wedded Sarah Murray, a half sister of Lieutenant Charles Cameron, of his own regiment, who was killed at Point Pleasant; and a full sister of Captain John Murray likewise killed in action; thus it was that the three were brothers-in-law, all of whom were killed. Major Thomas Posey, the Commissary-General of the Southern Division, had married the daughter of Sampson Mathews, Commissary of the Augusta Regiment, who was a brother of Captain George Mathews, commanding the first company of that Regiment. The former was therefore the father-in-law of Major Posey, and the latter his uncle by marriage. Colonel William Fleming commanding the Botetourt Regiment, had married Nancy, a sister of Colonel William Christian, commanding the Fincastle Battalion; and they were therefore brothers-in-law. Colonel Christian, and Captain William Campbell commanding a company in this battalion, had both married sisters of Patrick Henry, and were of course brothers-in-law. When Captain Campbell died his widow became the wife of Captain, (then General) William Russell, who commanded a company in the Fincastle Battalion, and thus he became a brother-in-law of Colonel Christian.

Captain Alexander McClennahan commanding a company in the Augusta Regiment, was a brother of Captain Robert McClennahan, of the Botetourt Regiment, the latter killed in the battle. He had wedded Margaret Ann, a daughter of Thomas Lewis, a brother of General, and Colonel Charles Lewis, both of whom were therefore his uncles by marriage, while he himself became the uncle of George R. Gilmer, a Governor of Georgia, and a brother-in-law of Captain John Lewis, of the Augusta Regiment. John Frogge, the sutler of the Augusta Regiment, who was killed in the first fire at Point Pleasant, had also married a daughter of Thomas Lewis, and was therefore a brother-in-law of Captain Robert McClennahan. After the death of John Frogge, his widow became the wife of Captain John Stuart, the Historian of Dunmore's War, who commanded a company in the Botetourt Regiment, and thus General Andrew and Colonel Charles Lewis became his uncles by marriage, annd Captain John Lewis, of the Augusta Regiment, his brother-in-law. Captain Evan Shelby who commanded a company in the Fincastle Battalion, had for his Lieutenant, his own son, Isaac Shelby; and Valentine Sevier, a sergeant in Captain Shelby's Company, was a brother of Lieutenant John Sevier, of Captain William Russell's Company of the Fincastle Battalion. Thus we might continue until it would be shown that the army which fought the battle of Point Pleasant, was largely composed of blood-kin men, and those related by marriage.

www.ingramcontent.com/pod-product-compliance
Lightning Source LLC
Chambersburg PA
CBHW072357030726
47505CB00014B/1872